Is this my beautiful life?

OTHER BOOKS BY JESSICA ROWE

The Best of Times, the Worst of Times: Our family's journey with bipolar (with Penelope Rowe)

Love. Wisdom. Motherhood: Conversations with inspiring women

Jessica Rowe

Is this my beautiful life?

A MEMOIR

First published in 2015
This edition published in 2016

Allen & Unwin
83 Alexander Street
Crows Nest NSW 2065
Australia
Phone: (61 2) 8425 0100
Email: info@allenandunwin.com
Web: www.allenandunwin.com

Cataloguing-in-Publication details are available
from the National Library of Australia
www.trove.nla.gov.au
ISBN 978 1 76029 402 1

Set in Minion by Midland Typesetters, Australia
Printed in Australia by Pegasus Media & Logistics

10 9 8 7 6 5 4 3

MIX
Paper from
responsible sources
FSC® C008194

The paper in this book is FSC® certified.
FSC® promotes environmentally responsible,
socially beneficial and economically viable
management of the world's forests.

For my mother and my girls for showing me how to love

'The only normal people are the ones you don't know very well.'

Alfred Adler

PROLOGUE

'Have you retired?' asks the bossy woman checking my parking ticket as I waited to drive out of the car park.

'Umm, no, I haven't.' I feel a little stunned to be put on the scrap heap so soon. 'I'm working part-time as a news presenter on *Weekend Sunrise* for Channel Seven. I'm also doing some public speaking, charity work and writing . . .'

'Who was that, Mummy?' asks my eldest daughter, Allegra, as the parking barrier lifts up.

Her little sister, Giselle, is busy squishing her favourite ball between her palms. She loves the glittery water inside, and the harder she squeezes it, the closer the orange clownfish goes to the plastic edges. She really wants to get Nemo out of his claustrophobic home. I spy what she is doing in the rear-vision mirror.

'If you keep doing that it will break. Then there will be no more sparkly water.'

She ignores me.

'Mummy, Mummy, who was that lady?' Allegra asks again.

'Oh, just the car park lady.' But as I say it, I think, wait a second – who *is* that? Why am I justifying, or feeling like I have to justify, my current situation to someone I didn't even know? That has been happening a lot. I often find myself giving my updated CV to the woman at the supermarket check-out, the pharmacist, the newsagent, the butcher, or anyone who asks.

And when I do so, I struggle to find a new title for myself. I am a crap cook, a sloppy housekeeper and a mother who still has her L-plates on. I deliberately let the clean clothes pile up in the laundry basket until they start to tumble out onto the wooden floorboards in the kitchen. Once that happens it is time to shift the basket behind the closed door of the 'study' that is really just a junk room. Only when there are no clean undies left do I finally start folding and putting the clothes away, stuffing them into the jam-packed drawers. This laundry procrastination is my personal protest over the domestic drudgery that takes up too many hours of my day.

My brain feels like it has turned into the playdough that I begrudgingly attempt to pick up when my little girls are in bed. I am sick of scrubbing the white Ikea highchair clean of banana, avocado and endless other pureed members of the five food groups that gather in every crevice. Do you know that you can puree spaghetti bolognese? I am jealous that other girlfriends with kids have flourished in their careers at the same time that I feel like I am going backwards. What am I doing wrong? I am a failure, and I am bored.

I am a mother. I love being a mother, but I also hate it sometimes. I don't hate my children, of course; I just hate what has happened to my life. I don't like being resentful, restless and stuck in a world of interrupted conversations, cold coffee and disrupted sleep. I am embarrassed to tell others I am a stay-at-home mum and proclaim that my children are the centre of my life. Weren't they? Sure, I am with them most of the time, but I also do part-time work. Being middle class with First World worries, I have enough money to pay for a nanny a couple of days a week. Our extended family also help to lighten the child-minding load on occasion. I know I am lucky to have a choice and that I should be grateful and happy.

Why am I so miserable, then? I loved my two daughters so much it hurt and cannot imagine my life without them. But no one told me it would be so hard. Am I the only one struggling? I see smiling, calm mums at the park, supermarket and school gate who seem happy to organise play dates and catch-ups at the park. Am I the only mother who hates play dates? It is hard enough keeping my two girls entertained, let alone supervising someone else's children, especially when they start fighting over whose turn it is with fashion fairytale Barbie.

My sister is one of those glorious mums who can run the house, chair the Parents and Citizens Association meeting at her sons' school and have meals organised each night. Why didn't we both inherit that organiser gene? It would have made my life much easier. Baked beans, pasta with Dolmio sauce and ten different ways with mince are my go-to meals. Am I the only fraud pretending everything is wonderful, and that I like nothing better than watching my girls on the trampoline when I'd rather be inside inhaling the entire season of *The Real Housewives of Beverly Hills* on the television?

In my pre-children and pre-husband years, I never imagined this would be my happy ending. I am proud to call myself a feminist, but am I really one when I look at the reality of my daily routine? The fairytale I have dreamt up sees me still blazing ahead with my career, sharing the cooking and cleaning duties with my husband, and having neat, tidy, brilliant and well-behaved children with beautifully brushed hair. But that is not my life.

My god, what had I done?

CHAPTER ONE

I first met my eldest daughter when she was a three-day-old cell. A smudgy, inky spot on a Petri dish.

'Is that your name on the bottom of the slide?' called the scientist through the door.

'Yes, it is,' I replied.

'Is that your husband's name?'

'Yes,' Peter said.

The sound of Peter's blue plastic chair dragging across the clean floor set my teeth on edge as we both gazed up at the grey, blurry outline being displayed on the wall-mounted television screen. I couldn't believe that this blur might grow into a baby, but I wasn't going to get too far ahead of myself this time.

Moments later, all that remained on the screen were spots of water as the scientist sucked up my 'three celler' into a pipette and brought it into the room, wisps of red hair escaping from her white surgical cap. As she checked our personal details again I nervously stumbled through our address and forgot our home phone number. We then had to identify our names on the pipette that was now safely holding our precious cells. That was something I could manage at least! I held my breath as the scientist carefully passed the pipette over to the doctor. Lying back slightly in the obstetrics chair, my feet were propped up in padded stirrups and a fine catheter had already been inserted through my cervix. As Peter squeezed my hand, I closed my eyes and said another prayer as Dr Tierney, our IVF specialist, transferred the microscopic contents through the catheter and into my uterus. It took sixty seconds. The watery potion was not yet an embryo, as the cells had to keep multiplying to get closer to becoming a new life.

'Is it alright to stand up?' I asked Dr Tierney, resting back on the green surgical chair. 'Or should I sit here a little longer?'

'You can get up—nothing will drop out!'

'Do I need to lie down when I get home? Do I need to stay in bed for the next two weeks before I get the blood test to see if I'm pregnant? Should I still stay off the coffee? Should I eat plenty of spinach? Should I—'

Dr Tierney gently interrupted my nervous blather. 'Jessica, try not to worry. Just keep doing what you have been doing. You don't need to stay in bed, but try not to put yourself under any more pressure.'

Peter helped me up and enfolded me and Dr Tierney in a hug.

'Thank you, thank you,' we said in unison. Peter and I clutched each other as we walked out of the tiny room and left the IVF clinic down the back stairs. It was the third time we had taken this walk together. Each cycle of treatment took around six weeks, from the first round of blood tests to the final embryo transplant. Initially I had believed modern medicine could guarantee me a baby, but it had now been over a year and I had forgotten how many prayers I'd whispered, pledging all types of promises if the IVF worked.

I had wanted to have a family for so long. My middle sister, Harriet, was already married to a fine man and they had a Botticelli baby boy called Chester. As the eldest sibling, I was panicked that time was running out for me. I too wanted that magical life, a handsome husband and cherubic children. Perhaps part of my yearning for a perfect life stemmed from the fact that the fantasy was far removed from my own upbringing. My parents divorced when I was young and I had seen my mother struggle to fill the fridge with food each week. Mum had her first breakdown when I was ten years old and was diagnosed with bipolar disorder when I was a teenager. Our family was far from normal, so I was determined to fashion a beautiful life for myself, the kind of life that I had read about in books and seen on American sitcoms, a life with a white picket fence. Even if that picket fence was going to be bedazzled with Swarovski crystals. Peter was the man for me: he was decent, dependable, kind and good-hearted. The sort of man I would have steered clear of in my twenties. Bad boys, playboys and deadbeats were top of the list while I partied the eighties away at Sydney nightclubs like the Cauldron, Kinsella's and Rogues.

As a seventeen-year-old I remember cranking up the boom box in my bedroom, singing along to the Cat Stevens classic about the big wide world I was desperate to leap into. The music would be super loud to drown out the traffic noise outside my window in our small flat, which was built right next to a busy road that had four lanes of traffic constantly charging up and down the hill. My thin bamboo blinds didn't block out the bright street light that illuminated my room all night. Those cheap blinds also weren't much good at muffling the sounds of the buses that stopped below my window, pumping their brakes, every thirty minutes.

In a polka-dotted midriff top that Mum had sewn for me, glossy cherry red lipstick and a short black ruffled skirt that spun out from my waist, I twirled dizzily until I fell over onto the prickly seagrass matting floor. The lyrics had become an anthem of sorts for me as I dreamed of escaping my narrow, small life. I was no longer a virgin and thought I knew it all, figuring I could get by with just a smile.

I had finished my last year of high school and despite studying hard I didn't get the marks I needed to study journalism at the University of Technology in Sydney. In the typically dramatic way of a teenager I felt like my brilliant career was over well before it had even begun. I decided a break from my routine would help me work out what I should do with my life. So I fled, although only down the road to a waitressing job in a fancy cafe. The equally fancy ladies who lunched there had no idea we were making their cappuccinos with one heaped teaspoon of Nescafé, a blast of boiling water and frothy milk sprinkled with cocoa. The milk steamer was the only thing that worked on the espresso machine, and it was obviously cheaper for the owner to stick with instant coffee than get it fixed. The short blacks must have tasted vile, three teaspoons of instant coffee that almost filled the tiny white cups. But that didn't stop them being popular—I guess some of the customers thought it made them look sophisticated, even if they couldn't drink them! I was quickly banished to the takeaway counter after I repeatedly muddled up coffee orders and dropped too many chicken caesar salads. And it was there that I met the ticket out of my boring life. He was over six feet tall, had a deep, raspy voice and ordered a mixed salad and a banana smoothie.

John also happened to be twenty years older than me, but I thought dating him would make me super sophisticated and sexy. Mr 37 was handsome, but he did have a saggy bottom. However, he owned a nightclub, a plane and a yacht. My mum banned me from seeing him, claiming he was a drug dealer and a sleaze. Of course I raged against her, yelling that she didn't understand and that I was in love. Then I did what all proper teenagers do: I ignored her demands and kept seeing my cradle-snatcher in secret. By then I had become good at subterfuge, organising to stay over with 'girlfriends' for the weekend when I was really meeting John at his nightclub and dancing the night away to Bryan Ferry.

My foolproof plan came undone when Mum discovered a bunch of photos (all G-rated). This was long before the era of selfies and sex tapes, but it did show me and Mr 37 on a weekend getaway. She was furious that I had deceived her, but even more concerned that the light plane we were travelling in (and John was flying) could have fallen out of the sky. In the bulletproof, arrogant style of a teenager, I told her not to be ridiculous. I knew what I was doing.

Mum realised she couldn't compete with my massive self-will so she stood aside, very unhappily, while I continued my inappropriate love affair with a much older man. Surprisingly, my dad and stepmother weren't as outwardly concerned, seeming to take the approach that it was better the devil you knew. A couple of times they came to dinner with us at the nightclub, me drinking Midori and lemonade while they stuck with wine, and we talked about scuba diving. Although it sounds terrifying to a parent, the actual experience was all rather mild and vanilla. I felt like an adult even though I still went home to sleep in my single bed most nights well before midnight. I never saw any drugs and was up early the next day to hit the gym with Mr 37. He was a health nut, so if we weren't training together we were mountain biking, water skiing or sailing.

I had taken a year off from studying, but after a while I knew it was time to knuckle down again and start at university. Although I had missed out on a place at UTS in Sydney, I had been accepted to study communications at Mitchell College in Bathurst. Moving to a country town a three hour drive west of the Blue Mountains was an enormous change for a city girl like me.

Not surprisingly, my new student life in the country wasn't a turn-on for my lover. He did fly there a couple of times, but I heard from friends that he was entertaining Swedish models on his yacht in my absence. Soon after that our affair ended and I was heartbroken, but not for long.

University was enough to distract me. I was majoring in broadcast journalism, and determined to become a star foreign correspondent. It was an ambition I had held since high school, and my new life, hundreds of kilometres from home with like-minded souls, was the first leap into the unknown that later became a pattern for my personal and professional life.

Towards the end of my studies I decided to take a year off and travel through Europe, funding my travels with a less than glamorous stint as an overseas catalogue model. Well before the internet, shopping by mail order was very popular, particularly in parts of Germany. These phone booked sized catalogues were full of cheesy looking photos of blonde models wearing fleecy sports tops and shiny, nylon leisure wear. The opportunity to star in these catalogues came up during the end of a long summer holiday from university. I was on the books of a Sydney modelling agency and a model scout was on her annual trip to Australia to find models suited to work in Germany.

She gave me a return ticket and an advance to cover four weeks rent for an apartment in Munich. All I had to do was turn up on the right date, start working and pay the agency back once I started earning Deutschmarks.

Originally I had planned to stay a month but once I walked into the modelling agency with my backpack and heard the different accents of the other newly arrived handsome young men and confident young women I knew I couldn't rush back home.

My wide world suddenly felt small again when I returned to Australia and university after a year overseas. The club escapades, snow-capped mountains and ancient cities I had managed to cram into those twelve months jarred with my draughty and grotty shared house in Bathurst. The piles of porridge-encrusted dishes that constantly filled the kitchen sink and mouldy tiles in a stinky bathroom that nobody ever cleaned were already getting me down. I wanted to run away again but Mum urged me to stay, explaining that most prisoners escaped from jail just as their parole was coming up, and I only had a year to go with my studies.

Once I graduated it wasn't long before I was on the move again, returning briefly to Sydney where I worked as a receptionist for the *Wide World of Sports* show on Channel Nine. A few months later I landed a job as a weather girl and reporter for Prime television in Canberra. I loved that job, learning about presenting and crafting a news story. However, after three years at Prime I was on the move again, this time to Melbourne where I worked as a journalist for *Nine News*. I lasted there for a year and six weeks until loneliness and homesickness finally dampened my wanderlust.

Home began to call me back. I missed Sydney's big bright blue sky and her footpaths strewn with fallen jasmine and frangipani flowers. But most of all I missed my family, who understood me best of all. I had spent much of my young adult life running away and wanting to 'grow up', but now I ached to be back in their embrace. I was considering a whole new career away from the media because I had become disillusioned working for *Nine News* in Melbourne. I wasn't cut out to be a daily news reporter. I didn't have the killer instinct to get the story regardless of the cost. I had no desire to camp outside people's front doors and try to interview them about the death of their child, husband or wife. I didn't want to get into strife from my boss because I didn't have a picture of the victim while our competitors had managed to get one from the family. I hated my job, and wanted to go home to Sydney.

However, the stars aligned one evening when I got the opportunity to read the news updates because the usual presenter had called in sick. Freakishly, the Network Ten Sydney news director, Mike Tancred, happened to be in Melbourne visiting his extended family when he saw me reading a sixty second update. The following week I got a phone call from Mike asking me if I would be interested in reading the *Five O'clock News* for Channel Ten!

'Ummm, well, I will think about it,' I told him, doing my best to keep a cool voice when all I wanted to do was scream yeeeess down the phone! He flew me up for an audition and I was offered the job later that afternoon. It was the biggest break of my career: the opportunity to co-host the main news bulletin for the Ten Network. At the age of twenty-five I thought I had finally made it!

I moved back home briefly, into my small bedroom that was still lit by the bright street light sneaking in under those same bamboo blinds. It wasn't long before I found a unit to rent at

Coogee Beach. If I stood on tiptoes on my balcony I could see the white bricks of the surf club. The smell of the sea air cleared my head and the salt spray smeared the windows of my new unit. Each morning I would drive into work to do updates through the day and then present the news from 5 to 6pm each night.

Initially I wasn't very good. I had a look of sheer terror on my face, like Bambi caught in the headlights. It was a miracle that my voice came out at all. I couldn't hear anything apart from the thudding of my heart. All I could see were the giant shoulder pads of my luminous lime-coloured jacket.

My father would leave a message for Ten's receptionist, Karen, after each news bulletin. He did this because Karen recorded every viewer comment to be then sent out to all the news bosses and station management the following day. Dad would try to put on a different accent for every call he made. However, it didn't take long for his cover to be blown.

'Hellllooooo, that girl in the bright jacket is very good . . .'

'Thank you sir . . .'

'Can you pass that on?'

'Yes sir and can I have your name please?'

'Yes, it's John Rowe.'

Dad kept calling though and Karen kept letting me know that he had left another message. Slowly, through practice, I improved my news presenting and had some extra voice training to work on my intonation and to make me sound more relaxed.

During those years I made sure I didn't get pregnant. I carefully used condoms, the pill and, if all else failed, the morning-after pill. My reckless sexual abandon was typical of a selfish and self-absorbed twenty-something, and it was probably helped along by the fact that Mum hadn't had an episode in hospital for a few years—it was time to kick up my heels and make up for lost time. For me, it was all about instant gratification and wearing the best shoes! I had no problems picking up the phone and asking a bloke out on a date as I had nothing to lose, and in my mind plenty to gain.

But on turning thirty my carefree smile was gradually replaced by a feverish, bunny-boiler, please-love-me look. Most of my girlfriends were married and had started their own families. I became tired of being the plus one at dinner parties and was even wearier of laughing off the 'what's a nice girl like you doing without a boyfriend?' comments. I wondered what was wrong with me. Was I too pushy? Too threatening? Too desperate? Yes, yes and yes.

Georgie, my closest girlfriend, was single too, and we spent many nights out together wondering if we would be left on the shelf. If that happened, we promised to retire together and buy a house in Perth with a fancy wraparound verandah, two ancient red-lipsticked ladies talking on our rocking chairs while casting our eyes over a pink Austin rose garden. In the meantime, Friday and Saturday nights had become our candlelit dinner-for-two dates. The pair of us spent so much time together that a gossip columnist speculated we had become lesbian lovers! We laughed at that while eyeing the seemingly shrinking pool of fellas propped up at Hugo's Lounge in Sydney's Kings Cross.

I was hopeless at playing hard to get. I gave my heart away too easily and too often had it thrown back in my face. And after spending a decade trying not to be pregnant, I'd gradually realised that I wanted to be a mother. The idea of a body clock was something I had ignored as nonsense, a conspiracy to stop women following their career ambitions. Now that clock was ticking loudly and I feared I had left it too late and my future would be me, myself and I, along with my tortoiseshell cat, Audrey.

My career was going along beautifully, at least, and I found myself all dressed up at the best parties, drinking the best champagne, but I had never felt lonelier. On one such evening I found myself glistening in gold sequins but stranded alone at the Logie Awards. My then boyfriend seemed to be hanging out in the toilet with some soapie stars, so I looked around desperately for someone I could talk to at the after party. Suddenly I was clinking champagne glasses with a very tall and charming man named Peter Overton. While he asked me lots of questions and patiently listened to my answers, I wondered why I was not dating a nice man like him.

'I like your style,' Peter said when he answered the phone a few weeks later. He wasn't surprised to hear from me because Tony, a mutual friend, had just warned him that I would be ringing.

'Why thank you,' I replied. 'Do you want to catch up? Go out to dinner?'

'Sure thing,' said Peter. 'If you like Thai food, there's a great place called Blue Ginger in Balmain.'

'I love Thai.'

'I'm going to Melbourne to do some interviews next week, so how about this Sunday night?'

'Lovely, great. Seven o'clock?' I'd decided there was no point stringing this out—there had to be more to life than a conga line of relationships and too many sauvignon blancs on a Friday and Saturday night. I had kissed a lot of frogs and was ready to find my prince and settle down. I rang Georgie to tell her that I was at last going out on a date with a proper grown-up.

Thankfully I was unaware that Tony had to convince Peter to take me out that first time. As I found out later, Peter was happy and busy in his new job reporting for *60 Minutes*, had finally recovered from his divorce and was enjoying 'playing the field' a little; he wasn't looking for another serious relationship. Tony told Peter that I would probably end up married to the local barrister, but I was feeling lovelorn and let down by men so just needed some cheering up.

Over stir-fried chicken with cashew nuts, Peter entertained me with tales of travelling the world as a reporter for *60 Minutes*. We compared stories about working in the media and I reminded him that we had first met many years before when I was doing work experience as a twenty-year-old in the Channel Nine newsroom. During dinner he made me laugh and feel comfortable because of the way he seemed genuinely interested in my life. It also didn't hurt that he had beautiful blue eyes and strong, broad shoulders. A few hours later Peter drove me home, walked me to my front door and kissed me chastely on the lips.

'Thank you for a fun night,' he said. 'I'll call you next week once I get back from Melbourne.'

As he said this, I involuntarily crossed my fingers behind my back. I sure hoped he was going to ring, but already I was preparing myself to be disappointed, having heard that line many times over the years. So I was surprised when, a week later, Peter called to ask if I'd like to catch up again in a couple of days. I explained it was my thirty-second birthday and I had organised dinner with my sisters, brother-in-law and close girlfriends. Peter replied that he would love to come along—if he was invited. I worked hard to keep the excitement out of my voice. Wow—he wants to get to know my family and friends. I knew this one was a keeper!

Peter and I were together for a couple of years before he proposed to me. Early on in our relationship I knew he was the man I wanted to marry, but he took his time. In fact, at one point we almost split up because I wasn't sure if Peter could commit to me. Understandably, he was gun-shy after the breakdown of his first marriage, but all the while my body clock kept ticking louder and louder and my ovaries would ache when I held the babies of my girlfriends. Would it ever be my turn? Georgie and I still had our regular date nights and lamented that life seemed to be passing us by. Maybe I was being greedy thinking I could have it all. I had a fabulous career, a glittering social life and a kind boyfriend. Perhaps children weren't going to be a part of my life.

One Saturday morning Peter left my unit early to help Mum move some computer equipment downstairs in her terrace. After waiting impatiently for her to open the front door, he exclaimed, 'You know, I've got more important things to be doing today!'

'Really? Like what?' Mum said, surprised by his uncharacteristic bluntness.

'Like picking up an engagement ring for your daughter!'

'Oh my god! Come in quickly—the computer won't take long and then go!'

Peter went to the jeweller to pick up the ring and then drove to my father's house to ask his permission. Dad agreed immediately, but Peter explained he was going to wait until next weekend to propose. However, Dad told him to ask me straight away, otherwise he wouldn't be able to keep his mouth shut! Like me, Dad loved a chat, especially if there was exciting news to share around.

Just as I stepped out of the shower I heard Peter knocking on my front door. Wrapping a towel around me, I didn't even have time to rub the panda bear mascara from under my eyes as I let him inside. Suddenly, he swept me into his arms in the narrow hallway where there was barely enough room for the two of us. Just as Peter started to speak I began to float above him, watching him hold me. I couldn't hear what he was saying as I was in shock, observing the scene from a distance. Wait a minute—did he just say what I think he said?

'Pussycat, you make me a better man. Will you marry me?'

I shot back down into my body. '*Yes!*' I screamed.

We married on a blindingly bright blue afternoon, the twelfth of January 2004, on a balcony overlooking Bondi Beach. As Peter and I exchanged our vows, the perfect wave was forming behind us. Squealing with joy, I threw my arms into the air and then around my new husband's neck as the reverend declared us married. We kissed on the lips, and as I opened my eyes, all I could see was Peter's blue, blue eyes. In his steady gaze, I knew the perfect life lay ahead for us.

We clumsily made our way around the dance floor. The pair of us pressed tightly into one another as the DJ played 'What's New Pussycat', our Tom Jones bridal waltz. Clutching the twinkling train of my dress, I leant against Peter's chest, even in heels only just reaching his chin. In that moment, under the moonlight, I had never felt safer, wrapped in my husband's arms. At last I had found my life partner, someone who I knew I could always count on, the man who would be there to look after me. As the rest of the bridal party joined us, I closed my eyes to imprint this moment into my memory. My good, golden-haired man would keep the vampires from the door. Everyone I loved, everything I needed, was sealed in this glittering, candlelit restaurant. Outside the full moon shone down onto the ocean, casting its blue, shimmery spell over us all.

CHAPTER TWO

Opening the curtains of our beach bungalow, all I could see was bright white sand. Once my eyes adjusted to the light I took in the palm trees lining our path to the beach, and under one of these were two dark teak beach chairs with a small table in between them. That would be our spot during our ten days in paradise.

'Petee, come on, get up! Oh my god, wait until you see this—it's so beautiful. Come on!'

A wondrous time lay ahead, starting with our honeymoon in the Maldives, where the azure water was luminous even in the dark. Soon after we got home from our beach bungalow overlooking the lagoon I stopped taking the contraceptive pill. Peter and I had talked for a couple of years about how we wanted to be parents. Now there was no time to waste: I was 33 years old and Peter was 37, and we were both ready to bring a new soul into the world and help her take fledging steps. Not that I knew I would have a girl, but secretly I hoped to have a daughter.

Women had been a strong force in my life. I had two sisters, Harriet and Claudia, whom I adored, and a mother who loved us fiercely.

Once our regular life began, so too did the plan to have a baby. Along with lots of sex, I prayed to the goddess, made a wish upon countless stars, read my horoscope and ate lots of leafy green vegetables, all in the hope of creating our own child. We had a huge mortgage with a perfect baby room set aside, but suddenly there was a glitch in our plan: at the age of 35, my body was letting me down. I was shocked at how hard it was to become pregnant. Naively I had thought that once I stopped taking the pill, my regular menstrual cycle would behave itself and my body, with a little help from my husband, would make a baby. I had imagined having a baby would happen quickly, easily and with little fuss. It was natural after all, wasn't it? However, each month when I saw the dark red blood on my white lacy underpants, I knew I had failed again. It was a personal failure. Everything I had previously wanted I had made happen through hard work and sheer force of will. This time my crash-through approach wasn't working.

The hormone specialist had diagnosed polycystic ovarian syndrome. It meant I didn't ovulate every period, and my body only produced a few eggs a year. There was no golden egg on day seventeen of my 28-day cycle. And there was no way of knowing which months were good for baby-making and which were rotten. Peter and I could keep trying and trying but time was against us. My husband's job as a reporter for *60 Minutes* meant he was away from home for eight months of the year.

His jet setting and my flawed biological clock had conspired to drastically reduce our chances of naturally conceiving a baby.

Everyone around us was pregnant or had young children. Jealousy and resentment sat heavily in my stomach each time a couple told us their good news. When Georgie, who had got married a few months before I did, told me she was expecting her first child, I was happy for her but upset it wasn't happening for me. Forget both of us being left on the shelf: now I was going to be the only one without a baby. The anger bubbled away inside of me. What was their secret? It seemed so unfair. I grew fearful it would never happen. Friends told us we needed to have a lot of sex, every day, and we just needed to relax. But when someone tells me to relax I get even edgier. And being uptight was not helping me get into the mood to have sex for breakfast, lunch and dinner.

Sex loses its spontaneity, joy and hotness when you feel like you are fucking to a timetable. And I didn't feel very sexy with my bottom elevated on a pillow just moments after Peter had come inside me; I had read, heard or maybe imagined that having your hips elevated keeps sperm inside you for longer, and those millions of little swimmers deserved the best chance they could get to meet the golden egg. All the research I had done consistently said that if you've been trying for a year to conceive, and for six months if you're 35, and you were still out of luck, then it was time for expert help.

So after twelve months of compulsory sex, damp pillow-cases, relaxation attempts and dirty weekends away and still no baby, Peter and I knew we needed to seek medical intervention, IVF. At the age of 35, my body was not following orders. I had assumed that being a woman also meant being a mother, so if I couldn't be a mother, what sort of woman was I? This aberration had never been a part of my plan. Despite well-meaning friends and family reassuring me that I would fall pregnant because they 'had a feeling', I was terrified that being a mother was never going to be part of my life. Did now switching to science mean that I was a cop-out? Was I being punished for wanting too much? Should I start investigating adoption?

Thankfully, our fertility specialist, Dr Raewyn Tierney, helped rein in my whirring mind with her practicality and kindness during our first appointment. She had a gentle face that oozed compassion, and her very presence said, 'But how are you—really?' Really, I wasn't coping at all, but I was well rehearsed in hiding behind the mask required by my job when I got into costume for my role of reading the news each night: designer suits, thick studio make-up and plenty of hairspray so nothing looked awry.

I couldn't look directly into Dr Tierney's brown eyes during the meeting, otherwise my tears would begin and never stop. A part of me wanted to drop my carefully manicured facade while I was there in her office but I still wasn't ready to reveal my vulnerability and desperation to her or to anyone just yet. Dr Tierney used her black felt-tipped pen to point to the simple diagrams on the pamphlet, clearly showing the different stages of treatment involved in IVF. Focusing on her explanation was a good way of keeping my increasingly anxious thoughts under control.

'And once we've got Peter's sperm we'll just tap the good ones on the head and team them up with one of your eggs,' Dr Tierney continued. My mind was full of information about drugs, blood tests, ultrasounds and injections. But the information I desperately needed was something the doctor was unable to tell us. All that mattered to Peter and I was whether the treatment would work. Would we ever have a baby?

The following Saturday, Dr Tierney gave us a tour of the IVF clinic where we would spend a lot of time over the coming months. I fixated on the ugly brown carpet in the reception area as we waited to enter the treatment room. Thankfully we were the last appointment of the day so we could look around without enduring the stares of other couples. I knew that if my desperation was mirrored in the eyes of another woman it would be my undoing.

Dr Tierney told us we could have our almost daily appointments (which would happen once we started a treatment cycle) before the clinic opened, and the nurses would let us in through the loading dock at the back of the building to avoid any possible media interest in our plight. The emergency exit stairs, our secret passage that linked the loading dock to the clinic, became very familiar to us during our quest for the golden egg and the golden child.

'And this is Di, she'll be looking after you,' Dr Tierney continued. 'She will do your blood tests, show you how to inject yourself with the medication and answer any extra questions you've got. Then once you've finished here, I'll show you the labs.' Di, the nurse, gave us a warm, calm smile, and Peter complimented her on her creamy pearl necklace. She had been working at the clinic for twenty-five years and had seen her share of nervous, emotional and desperate couples.

Peter and I sat down on uncomfortable office chairs. On the biscuit-coloured wall behind Di were dozens of photos stuck up with sticky tape of beaming couples snuggling brand-new babies, triumphant smiles on their shiny faces. Despite the many different families in the photos, each couple wore a similar expression of relief, joy and ecstasy. The blissful look said we have made it, we survived, and here is our reward.

It was impossible to concentrate while Di demonstrated how to use the injection pen, which was how I would self-administer the follicle-stimulating hormone each day. As she pushed the small needle into a rubber sponge I couldn't look, not because I was squeamish but because I had to study the happy family portraits on the wall. I thought by memorising their expressions it would help me to unlock their secret. How did they do it? How did they manage to have a baby? I must know. We sat on those bum-numbing chairs for an hour and a half while Di answered question after question from us.

'You'll have a picture of us to put up there. Please save a spot for us,' Peter said as tears streamed down his face.

'I will. There will be a spot for you.'

'How long will it take?' I asked. 'How long did it take for those couples in the photos?'

'Some of them had just one cycle of treatment. Others kept going.'

'For how long?' I persisted.

'As long as it took,' Di said.

Peter and I were taken through to the laboratory. 'The babysitting is going on in there,' said Di, pointing to a silver vat. And as she explained the process, I couldn't hold back my tears any longer. Inside each large cylindrical container were the hopes and dreams of so many couples, liquid nitrogen preserving their precious embryos. Each cycle of IVF treatment might produce more than one embryo, but the clinic would only transfer one at a time because of the health risks of having multiple pregnancies. Any extra embryos were stored in thin plastic straws, each one labelled with the couple's names and identification number, before being sealed at both ends and frozen. The embryo could then be thawed out if needed and transferred into the woman's uterus, rather than having to endure another full round of fertility treatment. According to the clinic, 30 percent of their patients had successful pregnancies using their frozen embryos.

Next we were introduced to the scientists in the lab. Two of them looked up from their microscopes. Dressed in blue gowns, with blue elasticised shoe covers and matching caps, the team were checking the health of the embryos under their watch. It had taken blood, sweat, tears and hormonal drugs to get the cells to this stage.

'Say an extra prayer for us when you see our names,' Peter said to the head scientist.

I kept my head down and looked at the white floor tiles, counting how many fitted across the length of the lab. I couldn't meet anyone's eyes, afraid I would burst into tears again. This was the only way I could stay in control.

Dr Tierney, Peter and I compared our diaries to work out the best time to begin our baby-making. It was encouraging to write down all the dates as it gave me a plan on which to focus my attention. I was frightened that my wafer-thin veneer might split and my supposedly successful, charmed life would come undone if I allowed my emotions to take over. In bright red texta, I drew a star on each date of the treatment cycle. Days to count down until my next blood test, days to count down until an ultrasound, days to count down until I had made enough eggs. Everything was clinical and planned, with no room for a spontaneous love child. It had to work.

When I first started using Synarel nasal spray, I welcomed the bitter aftertaste in my throat. Surely that meant the drug was quickly sinking into my system and flattening my hormones, shutting down my pituitary gland? The results of the first blood test would reveal whether my body clock had run out of tick and could now be manipulated by another dose of hormones. Once my body responded to the first lot of hormones, I was able to start injecting myself with hormones that would stimulate my ovaries to produce more eggs than usual. I wanted my body to create dozens of eggs to increase my chances of those eggs being fertilised, and then in turn increase my chances of becoming pregnant.

Listening to Di on the phone, I scribbled down the results from my latest blood test and ultrasound. The tests revealed how my body was responding to the hormones that were raging through my body. Again with my lucky red texta I wrote down *oestrogen at 3925, ten follicles—nicely**. I added the asterisk as my shorthand so I could remember to tell Peter that these results were promising. I continued making notes: *Stay on 75 today and Saturday and Sunday. Remember to return my admission forms, and to bring in an esky with an icepack, so I can keep my trigger injection cold.*

The trigger injection was a big and nasty syringe needle (different to the small injection pen I had been using daily) that I had to give myself the night before the egg-extraction operation, to prepare the eggs I'd been hothousing in my fallopian tubes. This injection replaced yet another natural hormone the body would usually produce when your eggs are ready to be released. If I went through each step methodically, properly and carefully, it would work.

Early the next morning, Peter and I arrived at the clinic ready for my egg collection. It was a Friday morning and I had taken the day off work for the procedure. I also wanted to have the weekend to recover before having to think about work again. Di pulled the curtain around my bed before I changed into a white surgical gown, blue paper slippers and a blue surgical cap. I was determined to walk into the operating theatre instead of being pushed through on the trolley bed. It was my small attempt to assert some control over a situation in which I felt I had almost no control anymore.

Once I had clambered onto the operating table, Dr Tierney told me to think positive thoughts. I tried not to look at the anaesthetist who was tapping my wrist to find a vein, but he quickly inserted the needle and gently asked me to begin counting down from twenty. I only managed to get to fifteen before the ice-cold oblivion of the anaesthetic took hold. During that time, Dr Tierney used ultrasound to locate my eggs and a long needle to carefully remove each one from my body. While that was going on, Peter was upstairs in a bland, beige-coloured room providing a fresh sperm sample.

The next thing I remembered was waking up with an oxygen mask over my face, groggily trying to read the number on the masking tape stuck to my wrist. I knew to look for it, as Dr Tierney had told me before the procedure about the precious white tape. In thin black biro it said *six eggs*. What, only six! Surely after all those drugs I should at least have double figures?

I lay there ruminating on the number six. Would that be enough? By the time the nurse came to check on me I was ready to interrogate her.

'Is that good? Or is it bad?' I asked.

'The doctor will be here soon, Jessica,' she said as she helped me out of the surgical gown and back into my jeans.

'But is six eggs enough? Is that what most women get? Or do most women get more?'

I sat down in an armchair and the nurse covered me with a heated blanket as I was shivery after the anaesthetic. While I was gulping down instant coffee and cramming a shortbread biscuit in my mouth, Dr Tierney came in.

I jumped in with my questions. 'Is six enough? I wanted to get more.'

'It's quality, not quantity, Jessica. We only need one good egg,' she replied.

After Peter drove me home I headed straight to bed, still feeling light-headed after the procedure and the first twinges of what would become nasty stomach cramps. Physically and emotionally I was wiped out, and withdrawing under the doona was the only way I could cope with the extra hormones swirling through my body. Drifting off to sleep that night, I dreamt of my eggs fertilising with Peter's strong swimmers. The embryologist would have chosen the most handsome-looking sperm and injected a single one into each of my six precious eggs.

By the time I woke up that Saturday, each delicate egg and sperm combination would be housed in their own incubators set at 37 degrees, a temperature that mirrors the human body. I tried to visualise each of those six cells flourishing. We had to get out of the house to kill some time before the afternoon phone call from the clinic about the state of our fledgling embryos. Peter and I walked slowly from our brick bungalow tucked in a quiet, Moreton Bay fig lined street to the sparkling harbour foreshore. Boats with bright red sails skimmed smoothly along the water. An old wooden ferry pulled into the wharf as tourists armed with cameras clambered excitedly aboard. A couple pushed a pram past while a jogger in zebra-striped leggings and a black singlet ran towards us. A normal, calm Saturday morning for everyone else, yet I had never felt so powerless and hopeless. There was nothing I could do to make sure our cells survived. There were no more dates or red texta stars to note in my diary. All we could do was wait for the phone call from the lab, and when it finally came later that day my mood plunged even lower. Only three of our six eggs had fertilised.

On Sunday, I couldn't leave the house, the machinations of everyday life jarring with my desperation. Peter went out to pick up a sweet, milky cappuccino and chocolate croissant for me while I stayed in bed. Again, the phone call from the lab later that day wasn't good: one cell had gone, another was starting to fragment and the final cell was hanging in under the watchful eye of the scientists. Dr Tierney recommended that we come into the clinic on Monday to transfer that fertilised cell.

'You have a beautiful eight celler,' Dr Tierney said the next day. Peter held my hand as the doctor inserted our eight cells into a narrow tube that had been inserted through my cervix.

'This is the best part of my job,' said Dr Tierney. 'Now think positive thoughts.' We gave her a hug as we walked back through the lab, thanking the scientists. They told us they hoped they wouldn't need to see us again. So did I. 'Hang in there, my darling eight celler,' I kept repeating to myself.

The two-week wait to have a blood test seemed to take a lifetime. The results of that test would reveal whether our beautiful eight celler liked my womb. Peter and I waited by the phone for the results from the clinic.

'I'm afraid . . .' started Di. Peter could hear her voice and was already crying. The two of us lay on the bed and couldn't move for the rest of the day. The bubble of hope that I had let blossom inside of me for those fourteen days had burst with a loud, ugly bang.

The experts—the doctors, scientists and nurses—don't know why the medication works for some women and not others. There is an unknown factor mixed in with the science and technology. I tried to deal with the void by praying, something I had not done in a long time. I wasn't sure who I was praying to but I hoped that someone, some higher being out there, would listen to my pleading lament. I liked to think it was a compassionate and glamorous goddess. Peter was more certain; he had a clear God in mind who he believed was listening to our prayers. I was willing to give anything a go if it meant becoming pregnant.

Six weeks later we were back at the clinic, and now I found myself glaring at those wretched happy family photos stuck on the wall of Di's office. It looked like a couple more pictures had been added since we were last here. Why were they lucky? Why did it work for them and not us? It wasn't fair! I'd given myself perfectly timed injections, turned up early for the blood tests and stopped drinking wine, but it was still not enough. I'd thought the miracles of modern science could guarantee me a baby—what about those Hollywood stars having babies well into their forties? I read about them often in the trashy weekly magazines I loved to buy. My doctor told me a lot of these older women were using donated eggs from much younger women. I didn't read that in the magazines; all I saw was the flawless star with her perfect baby.

Another fact I hadn't come across anywhere was that a woman is born with a finite number of eggs. For years I had been oblivious to the countdown of my own body clock, and now I only had old eggs left! I didn't feel old, but Dr Tierney said that in fertility terms, my 35-year-old eggs were pushing it. My remaining eggs were not as healthy as those I blindly bled away every month through my teens and twenties.

I psyched myself up, convincing myself that I'd cope with the second cycle of treatment better now that I knew how the heavy-duty cocktail of hormones would affect my moods and body. Work kept me busy. Before the news each evening I would hide in a toilet cubicle and take deep breaths. I'd quickly check no one else was in there before standing in front of the toilet mirror and saying out loud: 'I am talented, I am open, I am ready to communicate!' Each declaration was matched with a flourish of my hands to my reflection. If anyone was to walk in they could confidently say, 'Jessica, you are a lunatic!' Occasionally I was caught out and tried to disguise my affirmations with coughing fits. I hid my uncertainty with bravado, my acne (an unfortunate side effect of the drugs) with heavy make-up, and my bloated stomach full of hormones with looser pants. As I read the news on Channel Ten each night, no one could see the desperation and hope that was lurking behind my shimmery gold eye shadow.

But I couldn't keep up the facade when the clinic rang me at work to explain that I'd ovulated early, two days before the scheduled egg collection. Twenty-eight days of nasal spray, blood tests, injections and ultrasounds had all been for nothing. Dr Tierney explained that it was extremely rare and only happened in one percent of cases. Hiding in my dressing room, I called my boss and explained tearfully that I wouldn't be able to read the news that evening. Thankfully he didn't ask why and told me to look after myself. I drove home in a blur, not remembering how I made it to our front gate. Bed was the only solution and I hurried inside to bury my rage and grief back under the doona.

Dr Tierney suggested artificial insemination as a way of salvaging some of the stray eggs that may be floating around my faulty uterus after the unexpectedly early ovulation. Once again, Peter and I were back in the small room next to the lab, holding hands and trying to be positive. But we both knew it was a long shot so we weren't surprised when we got a call two weeks later to say that I was still not pregnant. The bubble of hope was now much smaller than when I learnt of that beautiful eight celler in our first cycle of treatment. I had relied on that bubble to deal with challenges in my young life. By nature I was a big believer in looking for the silver lining, but my optimism was struggling to even find a drab grey lining in this latest disappointment.

Peter and I still hadn't talked about what would happen if we couldn't become parents. In truth, I wasn't ready for my mind to explore that possible future. If I verbalised my fear that IVF would never work I worried that it would become a self-fulfilling prophesy. Previously I had discovered that if I committed to my career it would reap rewards. I was going to pursue this desire to become a mother, for us to be a family, with the same dogged determination.

To soften the heartache of the last failed interrupted cycle, we decided on a shorter round of treatment before Christmas. My weary ovaries were not responding to the higher levels of hormones I was injecting. Each morning at ten past eight, I injected myself with the now familiar follicle-stimulating hormone. It was satisfying to hear the click of the injection pen as I spun the dial around to the correct dosage. Getting up from the bed to dress, I would quickly glance at the five miniature 'lucky' Chinese cat statues I had on the table. Each porcelain figurine was no bigger than my fingernail but they had become my charms. The morning of my latest ultrasound to check on my follicles I decided to walk back to my mirrored bedside table to put the cats into a circle. My small circle of hope. I needed one good egg, just one.

CHAPTER THREE

'Happy birthday to you, happy birthday to you, happy birthday, dear Jessica, happy birthday to you!'

I love a party, any chance to celebrate. And this birthday was special. It wasn't just the fizzing sparklers on top of the chocolate mud cake and the satisfaction of making a wish as I plunged the silver knife through the thick icing that marked this evening apart. It was the chorus line of singers that made tonight especially memorable. I was being serenaded by my television idols. Superstar reporter Jana Wendt, who I had wanted to be when I grew up, was sitting next to me, and just moments before had been chatting about the decadent times she and her camera crew had at the Hôtel de Crillon in Paris while she was reporting for the *60 Minutes* program. All I could do was nod and smile, and hope that none of the chives from the seafood risotto we ate for dinner were stuck in my teeth.

The light from the sparklers reflected in the glasses of Brian Henderson, the legendary Nine Network newsreader. He held the hand of his wife, Mardi, while everyone called out 'hip hip hooray'. Also seated around the large walnut oak dining table was Mike Munro, a fearless journalist with a reputation for covering tough news and current affairs stories. Earlier in the evening he had asked how I coped with having my husband away for up to eight months of the year. Mike said he hated being away from his family when he worked on *60 Minutes*. I told him that my work at Channel Ten kept me busy too, and having time apart also meant Peter and I didn't take each other for granted. My dream dinner party guest list was finished off with the fabulous Liz Hayes. Here was a woman whom I had watched on breakfast television for years, and I was now hoping I could model my television career after her.

The ringmaster who had got us all together was the terrifying but oh-so-charming Sam Chisholm. He had me under his spell that night, recounting stories of superstars, billionaires and television. Most recently he had been working for Rupert Murdoch in Britain, where he had transformed BSkyB into a money-making venture for the media baron. In the eighties Sam had created the sparkling star system for the Nine Network by making household names of Ray Martin, Mike Walsh, Jana Wendt, Liz Hayes and Don Burke. He transformed Channel Nine into the number one television network during his time as managing director from 1976 to 1990. He famously coined the phrase 'winners have parties, losers have meetings'. Sam was now back at Nine as the acting chief executive after the abrupt departure of David Gyngell in May 2005. His brief was to find a new CEO and return the gloss and glamour to the Nine Network.

His gracious wife, Sue, kept our glasses of Cristal champagne full and made sure I was introduced to everyone. I tried to keep a check on how much I was drinking. I had never tasted Cristal before and it was tempting to quaff the heavenly bubbles too quickly. Two glasses had already taken the jittery edge off my nerves, but I wanted to keep my wits about me tonight and not end up slurring my words in front of this group. What was I doing in the middle of this stellar cast? Sam had called to invite Peter and me to dinner after we had filmed a mental health campaign. I was flattered to be in the company of a man who was famous for making stars in Australian television. I was still working at the Ten Network so there wasn't a job offer that night. But my ego entertained the idea that perhaps Sam would turn me into a star.

I had been reading news for Channel Ten for a decade. It was a job that I enjoyed, but after ten years in the role I was getting restless and ready for a change. I have always been a risk-taker. But was I ready to risk my stable, safe job and leap into the television big league? What do you think I wished for on the eve of my birthday?

Six months later I resigned from my job at Channel Ten. My contract was due to expire on 31 December 2005 and over that month I weighed up a new job offer from Sam Chisholm to co-host *Today* on Channel Nine. Peter and I were holidaying down on the South Coast when I decided it was time for a change. Peter was less sure that I should take the risk. He was already working for *60 Minutes* and worried that the both of us would be working for the same organisation. I've always been more inclined to leap into the unknown. My ego couldn't resist such an opportunity and it was now my turn to be in the limelight.

On 18 December I phoned Ten boss, Grant Blackley, to tell him of my resignation. He was disappointed but he respected my decision. I believed I was now free to sign a new deal with the Nine Network, which I did later that afternoon. I also phoned my close colleagues at Ten and they all told me they already knew of my resignation and wished me all the best.

I was therefore shocked to be served with legal documents through the front bars of our security door the next day.

'Ms Rowe, I'm under instruction to serve you with these legal papers.'

'No, no, I won't take them.'

'It doesn't matter if you won't take them, I can just leave them here on the front steps. I'm just doing my job, sorry.'

Taking the papers from the neatly suited man, I started dry-retching as I read: 'Channel Ten will be suing Jessica Rowe for breach of contract . . .'

Christmas was just two days away and in 2005 Sydney was enduring one of its hottest Decembers on record. Despite the air conditioning in my solicitor's office, the humidity left me stuck on his upholstered chair. I peeled myself off it for the unpleasant walk across town to meet with our barrister in his book-lined chambers. From there, seven of us walked together to the Supreme Court, with Peter and I leading the way. Flanking us were my wonderful solicitor, Joydeep Hor, and his two paralegals, followed by my wigged and robed barrister and his junior counsel. The streets we walked along were deserted, indeed the whole city was strangely quiet as everyone else had begun their summer holidays. While the rest of Sydney cooled down at the beach, we were sweating in our suits on the concrete footpath.

What a bizarre experience to be on the other side of the cameras. For years I had introduced numerous court stories and watched families walk the gauntlet of television cameras and journalists. Depending on the story I might feel sympathy or disgust for those in the report, registering emotions but in a disconnected, superior way. The walk to court that morning was a harsh lesson: I felt terrified, exposed and out of control. My fate, my future, was no longer mine but in the hands of competing legal minds.

While we waited for the traffic lights to change I spotted camera crews running towards us. I recognised the faces of the Channel Ten cameraman and sound assistants. Lindsay, who I had known for years, gave me a sympathetic smile before he pushed the record button on his camera.

'Jessica, how are you feeling this morning?' asked Amber, a reporter I knew well.

'Peter, this must be difficult for you,' said Ally, a young woman who worked at Channel Nine.

We had been advised not to say anything so I just kept walking, a steely look on my face and Peter tightly clutching my sweaty hand. But a closer look would reveal how wobbly I was under my clenched jaw and carefully chosen outfit. Head held high in my grey organza Zimmerman dress and matching jacket, I was in a state of high anxiety behind my carefully constructed facade. Only that morning, before court, I had received a call from the clinic explaining to Peter and me that our latest IVF attempt had failed. I was not pregnant. It had already been nine long months of disappointment.

There was no time to mourn the loss of our embryo yet as I had a public fight on my hands with my former employers. And I wasn't going to give up, not yet. Peter again squeezed my hand as I focused on walking up the steep courtroom steps. My legs felt shaky but I did not want to stumble in front of the cameras as I made my way up towards the entrance of the Supreme Court under the silver coat of arms of New South Wales.

Stilnox, caffeine and adrenaline got me through those insane six weeks. Cystic acne erupted on my cheeks, chin, neck and back from a combination of stress, leftover IVF hormones and humidity. A darling friend of mine, Nikki, who was a make-up artist, would come to my house early each morning to hide those ugly, painful blemishes with pancake-thick concealer. The paste-like foundation kept me glued together because I was determined to present an immaculate image. Now was not the time to fall apart as I had to show my new bosses that I was strong, capable and worthy of their investment.

My middle sister, Harriet, and her husband, Tim, were both solicitors, so they guided me through the maze of legal argument and procedure. During that stifling summer, from just before Christmas and all through January, there were three court proceedings. Network Ten claimed I had breached my contract and were intent on stopping me from starting my new job at Channel Nine, arguing that I had to give them 26 weeks' notice. This part of the proceedings took seven days. I listened to evidence from my former bosses, feeling outraged by their blasé recollection of events around my fate.

Sam Chisholm would ring me most evenings after I had met with the lawyers and give me a pep talk. I needed all the motivation I could get as I felt I had flown too close to the sun, wanted too much and that my fabulous new career was now in ashes. My favourite piece of advice from him, 'As Napoleon said, when you're faced with boldness, be bolder.'

And I needed to draw on all my boldness and bravery when it was my turn to be cross examined. I remember locking eyes with Justice Carolyn Simpson as I took my oath. Seated in the packed courtroom were Peter, my mother and step-father, my Dad and my step-mum, my two sisters and brother-in-law as well as journalists and Nine's legal team. Taking deep breaths, I listened carefully to the questions from Ten's barrister. My answers were calm and collected, and my voice sounded strong, even though my legs shook behind the witness box.

Two days later, Justice Simpson handed down her judgement, ruling that my two year deal would expire on 31 December. She dismissed Ten's argument that my contract was open-ended and that I needed to give 26 weeks' notice. 'The dispute between the parties involves one simply stated question—what is the expiration date of the contract. In my opinion, the answer is equally simple, derived from the terms of the contract itself, and favours the defendant.'

Justice Simpson also ordered Ten to pay my legal costs. She said Ten would have been in 'no doubt' that I was considering leaving, given I had requested new opportunities and refused an offer to replace Bert Newton as host of *Good Morning Australia*. When the verdict was read out, I turned and embraced Peter, thinking the stress and anxiety were now behind us.

But Network Ten appealed the Supreme Court decision and took me to the New South Wales Court of Appeal, the highest court in the state. Three judges unanimously dismissed the appeal with costs to be paid by Ten.

The legal bill totalled six hundred thousand dollars.

I won't bother going into the intricate legal arguments, which make my head spin even now, but I would not wish such an experience on my worst enemy. I don't believe my former employers wanted to keep me at the network. They simply used their court actions against me to try to make a wider commercial point to their competitors. The new chief executive officer of Ten, Grant Blackley, had just started in his role and my feeling was that he wanted to show the market that he meant business.

Personally, I was gutted to be used as a pawn; my integrity and professionalism were at the heart of who I was and how I had built my career. I also learnt the awful lesson that loyalty in the workplace is a myth, and regardless of how you conduct yourself there is a risk you will be used as collateral if the company believes it's in their commercial interest. But there was a bright side: I discovered how tough I really was in the eye of the storm.

After the final court decision, Peter and I were beaming as we walked out of the court hand in hand, my family by our side. Wiping humidity from my cheeks, I looked up past the silver skyscrapers and finally felt excited about the future that awaited me. I couldn't wait to start at the *Today* program in eight days' time.

My family, legal team, Peter and I walked past the Channel Seven studios at Martin Place, which were just around the corner from the court building. The lump in my throat from sheer relief got bigger when the journalists and producers in the Seven newsroom stood to give us an ovation through the glass windows. Things could only get better—or so I thought.

CHAPTER FOUR

Smiling, I tried to ignore the scratchy sanitary pads rubbing against my armpits. Mum had the ingenious suggestion of using them to absorb the copious amounts of perspiration I was producing. Unfortunately it wasn't working very well, but at least the watercolour print style of my wraparound dress didn't make the sweat stains too obvious. I just had to keep my arms firmly down by my sides and concentrate on each interview. Resisting my impulse to look too far ahead, I tried to focus on each segment of the show. I laughed while chatting with Bert Newton and later Dame Edna, our star guests that morning. Three hours later I could finally exhale: my first *Today* show was over. Feeling all eyes on me, I thought I had done okay.

Sam Chisholm rang me afterwards. 'A triumph, an absolute triumph,' he said. I breathed out a little more. Hopefully he could see I had been worth the effort and the court battle. It had to be plain sailing from now on, didn't it?

Peter and I decided to have a break from the IVF to give me a chance to focus on my new job. After a couple of months I was ready to find that bubble of hope within me again and we cautiously began another cycle of treatment. The smell of the fresh alcohol swab cleared my nose as I readied to rub it over a small patch of skin on my stomach. Quickly, I pinched a small fold of flesh between my thumb and forefinger and pushed down on the needle to let the hormone flood into my bloodstream. Squeezing my eyes shut, I imagined the drug fuelling the follicles in my ovaries. In an ideal world the follicles, which is the sac of fluid surrounding each egg, would multiply. So the more follicles, the more eggs. If the egg matured, the alchemy of magic, medicine and miracle would bring me one step closer to having a baby.

Everywhere I looked there were babies. Mums nestling their newborns in slings wrapped across their chests, twins in strollers, mobs of mothers pushing their prams along the footpath while I stepped into the gutter to get around them or to get to the barista at my local cafe. 'Baby on board' stickers were on the back of every car that stopped in front of me at traffic lights. Even worse were the stickers of a mother, father, baby and dog. Wickedly, I was tempted to drag my keys across the paint of family wagons with those white stick-figure images stuck on the back window. Begone with your smug stickers! Stop flaunting your breeding abilities in my face!

My hackles were already up when I spotted more of these stickers one Saturday morning. Peter and I were driving back from the clinic after having another blood test to check how my hormones were responding to the medication. My hormone levels still weren't right and I was flattened by the latest setback; the delay didn't fit in with the carefully crossed out dates and strategic stars I had written using my 'lucky' red texta in my diary. Stupidly, instead of relying on my guaranteed mood lifter of soft-centred strawberry cream chocolates and going back to bed, we stuck to our plans.

'Can't we just cancel? Can't you ring and tell them I'm sick?' I complained, glaring at the smiling stick figures on the car in front.

'But you're not sick! We told them we're coming.' Peter's insistence on not letting people down meant there was no escape from Marissa's first birthday party that morning. Normally I loved the decency of my husband, and we often joked about him being my PA as I was hopeless at returning phone calls and sticking to plans. However, this morning I was in no mood for jokes or first birthday parties, no matter how sweet Marissa was.

The frantic jumping castle, melted chocolate crackles and polite conversation did nothing to help my mood.

'Hurry up, you two,' joked one of the party guests as the conversation inevitably turned to baby-making. 'What are you waiting for?'

I wanted to scream, 'I'm on IVF and I don't know if I can be a mum. I have just come from having a blood test to see if my body is responding to the hormones I'm pumping through my body. Don't tell me how wonderful it is to be a mother! And don't you dare complain about how tired you are.' I wanted to tear the pink princess jumping castle apart and tell the women what they could do with their sleeping routines, controlled crying and pram debates. As I listened to them I made a promise never to bore people with endless stories of my children. I would never whinge, complain or find it difficult once I had my precious child. I would know how hard fought it had been to have a baby. Didn't these mothers realise how lucky they were?

My raw anger took me by surprise. Usually calm and considerate, now I was ready to rip people's heads off. The hormones I was flooding myself with had turned me into the Incredible Hulkess.

Every couple of days I had an appointment with Di, my nurse at the clinic. Yet another needle would pierce my skin to take blood and check my hormone levels. It was satisfying to write down these appointments, one small thing I could document and control. During the two weeks of hormone treatment I had regular blood tests and ultrasounds to see how my follicles were responding to the fertility drugs. Towards the end of that time, Di told me that the ultrasound was looking good. As she pointed out the black and grey images I imagined that my follicles looked like fine seaweed, delicate tips enfolding round, shadowy seeds. My eggs were ripe and ready. I just had to give myself a large injection before bed that night to trigger my eggs out of their mermaid home. I was excited about having a general anaesthetic; an operation was something else I could mark down in my diary.

The next morning at the clinic Dr Tierney told me once again to have positive thoughts as she prepared to remove a batch of eggs from my hopefully jam-packed ovaries. I stared at the needle as it slid into my wrist, embracing the oblivion that sped through my veins. Desperate to have time-out, to hand responsibility over to the experts, I let go. I wanted relief and obliteration.

It didn't last long, and in my next conscious moment I was lying in recovery on a narrow surgical bed, struggling to bring my right hand to my blurry eyes. I needed to know what my plumped-up fallopian tubes had delivered to me this cycle.

Written in thin black biro on a torn piece of masking tape stuck on the top of my hand were two words: *eight eggs*. It was the third time I had woken up in this recovery ward and I felt safe hidden behind the blue curtains pulled around my metal bed. I recognised the familiar stirring of hope, excitement, dread and desperation as I stared at the cream-coloured tape. The number written there held my hopes for a family, eight more chances to create a new soul. Eight chances for the scientists to inject my husband's sperm into my ageing eggs. I slipped down the oxygen mask that still covered my face and pressed the scrappy masking tape to my lips: please let it be this time.

At ten past ten the next morning, my mobile rang. It was Liza from the laboratory. 'You're doing well. Six of your eggs have fertilised. We'll ring you again tomorrow and let you know how they're going.'

'Oh thank you—that's wonderful news.'

The next day I sweated by the phone, wondering what was taking so long. Had something gone wrong? When my mobile finally rang I snatched it up quickly. It was Liza again.

'You have five left, but two have started fragmenting, so that leaves three that are looking quite good.'

'Quite good?'

I was desperate for more reassurance, but unfortunately Liza couldn't give me any. Dr Tierney called in the afternoon to explain the plan of action. She said if the three remaining embryos weren't doing so well tomorrow she would transfer one of them into my uterus around lunchtime. Apparently they had a better chance of surviving inside of me than in a Petri dish. Di also rang to check how Peter and I were coping. Her kindness made me want to weep. It was hard to stay balanced with the huge amount of hormones that were still sloshing around my body. We had chosen not to tell our family that we were going through IVF again—it was too hard to manage their hopes and expectations along with our own emotions. Earlier failed attempts had left me heartbroken and angry and I couldn't keep repeating the story, explaining the medication and the treatment.

However, there was one person I did tell about our third IVF attempt: my girlfriend Annebelle. Without intruding or constantly asking how the treatment was going, Annebelle was just there. I loved that she was into chakras, the moon and magic. She was preparing a spell for our inky black smudge, lighting three pink candles with three pink flowers. I was not convinced by the pretty potion, but I was prepared to believe in unicorns if it meant becoming a mother.

The next two weeks until a blood test would reveal whether I was pregnant took an eternity. I had allowed the bubble of hope that I carried to get a little bigger. Perhaps those three little cells I saw on the screen had now developed into a blastocyst. Perhaps the embryo had now embedded itself into the wall of my uterus. Perhaps it was flourishing. Or perhaps it had shrivelled away. Just a day after the transfer, Peter had to fly to Italy for a *60 Minutes* story on Formula One racing. His constant travel had begun to wear me down. Lately we seemed to have an argument just before he went away and then when he first came home. Our conversations also seemed rushed and incomplete before he had to zip away on a story. All I wanted was to cling on to him tightly and have him close by as we tried to make sense of what was happening. Now I only had myself and hopefully my growing embryo for company. At least work was a distraction.

There couldn't have been more of a distraction than that festival of insincerity, the TV Week Logie Awards. The Australian television industry's awards evening broadcast from the Crown

Palladium in Melbourne was always full of glitter, sequins, fake smiles and fake conversations. But I loved being a part of it, loved the chance to dress up and feel rewarded for the hard work I had put into my career. This year I would be hosting the red carpet arrivals show to be broadcast before the awards. After being shown up to my hotel suite on the executive level of the Crown Towers Hotel, I stretched out on a grey velvet couch and rang room service to order a club sandwich, my hotel room staple, before my gig for the evening began.

'Ladies and gentlemen, welcome to the forty-eighth annual TV Week Logie Awards red carpet show. I'm Jessica Rowe, and tonight you'll see all the glitz and glamour from our biggest stars.' I was wearing a floor-length, silver-sequinned Collette Dinnigan gown. The make-up artist had expertly covered the acne that continued to plague my face and back, an ugly side effect of the IVF. I was interviewing my colleagues on one of the highest-rating television shows of the year, but the best part of the evening was the secret I was carrying inside my watery womb, shielded from the flashes and bright lights. It was easy to avoid the champagne without attracting any suspicion. My excuse, that I had to get up at 3am to co-host *Today*, satisfied my workmates. Nothing was going to jeopardise the chance of this nine-day cell growing, and growing. I could cross off another day in my diary—only ten more days until I knew if I was pregnant.

The phone rang at 12.45pm; Di was punctual as always. I let it ring a few more times. I wanted to hold on to hope for a little longer.

'How are you?' asked Di.

'I'm beside myself,' I replied.

'You don't have to be any longer—you're pregnant.'

'Oh my *god*, I can't believe it. Thank you, thank you, thank you!' I screamed and cried at the same time. Hot, happy tears streaked down my face as I jumped up and down in the empty living room. 'I have to ring Peter.'

It was 3.10am in Milan. Peter had been lying in his hotel room staring up at the white stucco ceiling, waiting for the phone to ring.

'Petee,' I screamed, 'you're going to be a father! I'm pregnant!' We sobbed down the phone line together.

Saturday morning bliss. I rolled over to check the time, dislodging my old tortoiseshell cat, Audrey, who had taken to sleeping curled up against my stomach. She knew something was going on, and I wondered if she could sense Milano blossoming inside of me. Peter and I had nicknamed our baby in honour of the place Peter was working when he discovered our glorious news. Our Milano was now five weeks old and the size of a chocolate chip.

It was already nine o'clock and such a treat to still be in bed, with no alarm going off at 3.20am. I had been getting up at this nightmare hour for a couple of months and still I was not used to it. Do you ever get used to getting up in the middle of the night? I have never been a morning person and here I was hosting a breakfast television show! Several times I'd stumbled into the shower unaware I was still in my cat-print flannelette pyjamas until they were soaking wet. Every weekday morning

I drove in the pitch-black across the Harbour Bridge, the lights of the city reflected on the oily, dark water as I made my way to the television studios. The roads were deserted apart from a few taxis, hire cars, garbage trucks and couples staggering home from a big night out.

Each evening bedtime was between 8 and 8.30pm, something I hadn't managed since I was a little girl. This left enough time to read through my briefs, the background information for the interviews I'd be doing the next morning, and watching *The 7.30 Report* on ABC television before I went to bed. All work and no play was turning me into a very boring girl. At least with Peter travelling constantly for his reports on *60 Minutes* it was not as if we had a 'normal' existence anyway.

'How good is bed?' I asked Milano and Audrey, as the cat curled back into position next to my tummy. And I planned on staying put under my soft sheets for most of the morning. Peter was away so often that I was used to spending time either on my own or with my mother or sisters to fill in the days. I thought that perhaps Mum and I could go to the movies. We had a lot in common, including our taste in films—which was just as well, since Peter was more interested in rom-coms and there are only so many Jennifer Aniston movies I can manage.

Stretching my legs out in our king-size bed, I was considering getting up to bring the newspapers inside to check the movie times when I felt something damp between my legs. At first I thought I was imagining it. Audrey jumped off the bed and flicked her tail as I sat up, swinging my legs down onto the wooden floorboards before quickly pulling down my pyjama pants. There were coppery brown bloodstains. 'No, no, no, *no*!' I screamed. Grabbing my mobile off the bedside table, I frantically searched for Di's mobile number.

'Di, I'm so sorry to call on a Saturday, but I'm bleeding. I don't know what to do. I can't lose this baby . . .'

'It's okay,' said Di in calming tones. 'Is Peter there?'

'No, no, he's away, in Uganda.'

'How much bleeding have you had?'

'I'm not sure, I don't think I'm bleeding at the moment.'

'Alright. Can you get your mum to drive you into the clinic and we can do a blood test to see how everything is going?'

'Am I having a miscarriage?' I had to say my deepest fear out loud.

'Just call your mum and get her to bring you in. We can talk once you're here.'

Back at the clinic, Mum held my hand while Di explained that it was normal to have breakthrough bleeding, but she wanted to make sure my hormone levels were still up. If these levels were increasing it meant I was still pregnant. Bright red blood drained quickly from my arm into the phial, but I couldn't look away from those happy family photos stuck on the wall.

Di gave me a hug and told me to go home and relax, and she would phone with the results on Monday. How could I relax when my mind kept lurching from hope to catastrophe? I dropped onto the couch, the very same spot I had been when Di phoned with the wonderful news four weeks before. Frightened of where my mind would go if left to its own devices, I kept replaying my conversation with Peter when I shared our news. When that didn't work I began counting the books on the bookshelf, counting the number of shelves, the number of titles with pink writing on the book spine, the number of books that were mine, the books I had nicked from Mum, Peter's sports biographies—anything to stop me from falling off that cliff and shattering into pieces. It was a fall I had taken when Peter and I learnt that our first round of IVF treatment had failed and I didn't know if I could take it again and survive.

Audrey jumped onto the couch and curled herself against my stomach, purring as I stroked her soft, fluffy fur.

'Oh Auds, you understand, don't you, my darling,' I whispered.

Bits of her motley coat were coming off onto the white mohair rug I had tucked around myself. One, two, three, four, five, six, seven, eight, nine, ten, eleven, twelve—now I was counting the hairs she had shed on the rug. I could not lose my baby. I could not. Do not give up, my precious. Hold on, I promise I will always be here for you. I love you, I love you, I love you. Oh how I want you. I need you.

This baby was my salvation and my strength, and the secret of conceiving her had kept me going through those months in my new job co-hosting *Today* on the Nine Network. It was a job that I loved, but it was also causing me such heartache and humiliation. On only my second day as co-host, I had woken up to headlines likening my appearance to a velociraptor. Remember those skinny, mean-looking dinosaurs that were the villains in *Jurassic Park*? The columnist said I had 'razor sharp, short blonde hair', and described my chemistry with co-host Karl Stefanovic as 'thrusting a hand towards her co-host like an over-friendly raptor'. The article concluded with the line, 'It had been three hours, but it felt like three years.'

The words hurt, even though I expected to be criticised. Not everybody was going to like me, but I'd always worried far too much about what people thought and had wasted too many years seeking their approval. Constructive criticism wasn't a problem as I understood I had much to learn. But what wasn't helpful was the personal denigration that dominated much of the media coverage. My intelligence, appearance, weight and loud laughter were frequently called into question. One commentator summed me up this way: 'Rowe has the long limbs and angular face of a model; she is childless and loud.' All eyes were on me in my new role and I had a lot to prove, not only to myself but to my former colleagues and new bosses. However, now I didn't care if my career was taken away from me; all that mattered was my Milano. But if I lost her, my sweet secret, I knew I would be broken.

CHAPTER FIVE

The phone rang; it was Di.

'It's okay, your blood levels are good. You are still pregnant.'

My Milano was already a determined soul, and her doggedness gave me the energy to keep turning up for work each morning and standing tall, despite continuing cruel media comments.

Over the next few weeks I enjoyed the way my body was softening and stretching. For the first time in my life I had hips and breasts, and I marvelled at how my boy-shaped physique, straight up and down like an ironing board, was filling out, plumping up and ripening like a soft, lush peach. In the shower I would run my hands over my newly rounded breasts, revelling in their shape and size. At last I had a line of cleavage between my boobs without even trying! In the past I would have had to wrap my arms right around my body then lean forward to even get a hint of a bust.

Twisties and hot chips became my breakfast of choice. I relished lamb cutlets or fillet steak for dinner, quite a change for someone who hadn't eaten cuts of meat in about ten years. Previously I had been a peculiar type of not-quite-vegetarian, someone who occasionally enjoyed indulging in sausages and bacon. My youngest sister, Claudia, who was a chef, always teased me about this weakness for the worst kind of meat on the menu.

Now I understood the pleasure of eating the right sort of meat, chewing tender crumbled cutlets and savouring their sweet flavour. The perfect match for this meal was mashed potato, softened with knobs of butter and a generous slurp of cream. At dinnertime—or at any time, really—I devoured my food faster than my husband, quite a feat given his lifelong ability to hoover meals in a matter of minutes. My stubborn, angry acne finally cleared up now that hormone injections were a thing of the past and I had the sort of glowing, dewy skin I'd only ever read about in the magazines. At long last, I had become the clichéd pregnant woman. Nothing was going to break my stride—which was just as well, because my career was on skid row.

Although I understood that a certain level of scrutiny went with a high-profile job, what I couldn't understand were the relentless personal attacks. One morning after work I was sitting on our front steps, getting some sunshine before I logged on to the computer to check the rundown for the next day's show. I opened an envelope in my stack of work mail that was full of clippings from a Melbourne newspaper paperclipped to a note written on an old typewriter. I should have thrown it away the moment I saw the typed letters on faded yellow notepaper, some darker than others depending on how hard the typewriter keys had been hit. In my favourite TV crime shows, an oddly typed letter is a giveaway that the writer is a little unhinged, maybe even a serial killer. But instead I read the letter, full of such hate for me, my laugh, my short hair, my weight and my life. I was dumbfounded that someone I had never met could write such cruel and vicious words. The attached newspaper clippings were nasty letters from other people who had been invited to write in about me by Melbourne's *Herald Sun* newspaper. These criticisms had been highlighted with yellow fluorescent pen by the author of the typed note.

I'm sure this kind of pressure caused me to have another pregnancy scare. Early every morning after I got up I had been checking for blood, then just after 9am when the show had finished I would be back in the bathroom to check again. However, my heart stopped one Wednesday morning, when I saw an ugly red discharge on my undies. I grabbed my phone.

'Di, I'm bleeding again. I don't know what I'll do if I lose this baby!'

'Jessica, please stay calm,' Di soothed. 'I'll organise an ultrasound for you this afternoon to check that everything is okay. Try not to panic—it could be from the pessaries you've been using to help your uterus provide the perfect hormonal conditions for your baby.'

Peter came with me to the clinic and helped me onto the bed. Neither of us could speak while the sonographer spread the gel on my stomach and then placed the probe on top to capture the soundwaves that might tell us what was going on.

'There's a heartbeat,' she said.

'A heartbeat—a heartbeat!' said Peter and I in unison.

Desperately I marked off each day in my diary, willing the weeks to whizz by in record time. Instead it had the opposite effect and each day was like wading through thick, syrupy treacle, slow and frustrating. I never expected to be so anxious. I had imagined that once I discovered I was pregnant that would be it, I would have made it. Now I realised how tenuous the little soul was inside of me and I whispered to her every moment I could to stay with me. Hang in there, my Milano.

Still I kept setting the alarm and showing up for work while the rest of the world slept. On camera I smiled and laughed and tried to be myself, even though a producer had suggested I needed to stop laughing. Initially I bristled at the idea: was I really as bad as everyone was saying and writing? Was I a joke, a fraud? How could I keep being myself and feel confident when I had to second-guess everything I did and said? My laughter was intrinsic to who I was; I had always laughed long and loud. My parents and then my teachers had failed to smother my noisy laugh and even my tendency to snort when I found something especially hilarious. Laughter had been my defence mechanism, the antidote to dealing with challenging times. And now that weapon had been taken away from me. I stopped laughing on camera.

Before I had accepted the job I told the head of news and current affairs, Mark Llewellyn, that I was worried about my lack of interviewing experience. He reassured me that I would get plenty of backup from producers so I would never feel underprepared going into the studio. During my first week I interviewed the then prime minister, John Howard. I was nervous but did my research and felt good about how it had gone. Each day I learnt something new, and I enjoyed feeling intellectually stretched each morning.

But while my brain was enjoying new challenges, my body was still defying orders as sweat continued to pour out of my armpits. I tried everything to hide the wet patches under the arms of my brand-new Armani jackets. I'd given up on using sanitary pads and in the end just kept my arms clamped even more firmly by my sides. I wanted to relax in my role but still felt under the microscope.

'Don't wear that pink jacket again,' the producer said after one show.

'What?' I replied, stunned.

'Eddie hates it, don't wear it again.'

'Oh—okay.' I was used to having my clothes and hair commented on, having worked in television for ten years. Such scrutiny on your exterior appearance is an occupational hazard for women in the media.

The jacket went to the back of the wardrobe, but I felt under increasing scrutiny. After one show the whole team were summoned to the office of Nine's chief executive, Eddie McGuire. Just a few weeks before, Eddie had been appointed the CEO of Nine after starring on our screens for years on *The Footy Show* and *Who Wants to be a Millionaire*. He was also credited with turning around the fortunes of the Collingwood Football Club. I couldn't look anyone in the eye and started studying the sharp edges of the ugly marble coffee table in the middle of the office.

I could take constructive criticism but it was awful having such a discussion in front of all of my workmates. Thirty people sat around watching the interview while I tried to make myself as invisible as possible. I wanted to click my heels and disappear in a puff of perfumed smoke. Eddie then asked the group to tell him what was wrong with the interview and what I should have done. One of the junior production assistants put up her hand and announced how she would have handled it, something

I would never have done when I'd been an assistant. That marble coffee table was looking like a better and better place to hide under.

The pressure increased after an interview I did with Brigadier Michael Slater in East Timor in May. Australian troops had been deployed to Dili to help return order to the streets after rioting had left 200 people dead. The East Timor president, José Ramos-Horta, called on Australia, Portugal and the United Nations to intervene in the crisis, and Australia sent peacekeepers to the region. I began the interview with my background notes in front of me on the desk, and as usual I had an earpiece in my left ear, so the producer could talk to me while the show went to air to suggest questions, give me information or tell me to wind up the interview. It was a useful way to communicate without interrupting the flow of the interview and program.

Brigadier Slater appeared on the satellite dressed in his army fatigues, two armed soldiers behind him. The time difference meant it was still dark in Dili, but it was light enough to see the weapons the soldiers held in their arms. I could also see the fronds of a palm tree over the brigadier's shoulder. The interview started with me asking Brigadier Slater about what conditions were like in Dili at the moment. Before long, I heard the voice of the producer, in my earpiece. 'How can it be so safe with those soldiers behind him? Ask the question, Jess,' he said.

The brigadier was in the middle of his answer outlining the situation for Aussie troops, so I let him continue.

'Ask the question, Jess. The question!' the producer persisted.

I kept listening to the brigadier.

'Jess, you have to ask him to justify why he is saying it's safe when he has those soldiers behind him. Ask him, ask the question!'

I relented and asked the question. 'Looking at some of the pictures we've been seeing there, it looks incredibly chaotic. It doesn't look safe on the streets—there are crowds there lining up, desperate for food—and I'm wondering how you feel about your safety given that you've got armed guards there behind you, armed soldiers.'

'Jessica, I feel quite safe, yes, but not because I've got these armed soldiers behind me that were put there by your stage manager here to make it look good,' the brigadier replied. 'I don't need these guys here.'

I quickly apologised, explaining that I was unaware this was the case and continued with the interview. The producer who had been insistent that I ask him about the armed soldiers was unusually quiet in my earpiece. Later that day when articles started appearing online about the interview, I suggested to my bosses and the publicity department that we needed to respond to the criticism. I was told I was overreacting.

The next day I was pilloried on radio and in the newspapers. My unheard defence was, of course, that I was totally unaware the shot had been set up by our team. I had a producer in the control room in Sydney insistent that I ask the question, and another producer in Dili who had staged the background to look more appealing for television. However, neither producer had communicated with the other about what was happening. Of course, I realised the buck stopped with me, but I felt like I was being hung out to dry.

Since then I have been made aware that the brigadier did in fact travel with those two armed soldiers and it was a regulation that army personnel were to be accompanied by two armed soldiers if they left the compound in East Timor. However, when I found this out the damage had long ago been done.

Every Sunday I would anxiously read the newspapers as there was always something written about my precarious position on *Today*. Okay, I knew my public profile meant I was considered 'fair game' by gossip writers, I could cop that, but their unrelenting focus was beating my usual optimism out of me. Even Mum's attempts to cheer me up with the 'at least they're writing about you, darling' line was losing its shine.

Peter was more hurt about the commentary than me. He was desperate to protect the person he loved and on occasion told me he would talk to management to try to sort it out. I was more cautious as I didn't want to jeopardise both of our careers so suggested that he hold his nerve. Peter did talk to his boss John Westacott about our IVF treatment. John was supportive of both of us and he managed Peter's travelling schedule so he would be home for the important times in the fertility cycle.

But when Peter was away, travelling for work, he tried to read the weekend papers online before I had a chance to see them. That way he could call me first and talk through any of the unpleasant stuff. Thankfully he was home on the Sunday morning when a large paparazzi picture of myself and my stepfather was published with an accompanying article. The photo showed me holding hands with a clearly frail older man as I helped him to cross a busy road. We had just been at a cafe and it was one of the last times he was able to walk out of the house because this wise, kind and clever man was being robbed of his dignity by dementia. And now here he was, disrobed in public to be used as a cheap punchline in a column about my job insecurity. I raged at my executive producer that I could cope with the unwanted attention but my family was off limits. Although I made it clear how upset I was there was nothing I could do to stop such articles.

Once again I turned up at work the next day smiling, and once again no one said anything to me about what had been written in the paper. The show must go on, so I kept up the brave facade. Often my good nature has been confused with being too nice or an easy touch, but I was no pushover. In fact I was plain stubborn, plus I was determined to do the job I had been paid to do. I had spent fifteen years building my career and I was not going to give it up without a fight. For me that didn't mean making a loud fuss but being professional, dignified and true to myself.

Just when I thought the latest storm had passed and I might be left in peace, something else would be written in the newspapers. I was chastised in one paper for turning up late to Nicole Kidman and Keith Urban's wedding; it simply wasn't true, but that didn't stop it being written. During that glorious wedding, I had a chance encounter with the uber-publicist Wendy Day, who from that night took me under her wing and kept me there. This fuchsia-lipsticked, warm and fierce woman helped me navigate the very ugly media storm that kept whirling around me.

At last there was someone in my corner.

Laughter bounced off the wooden floorboards of the boutique pub, the crush of people and the dodgy acoustics making it hard to hear anything. A big group of journalists and producers had got together to farewell Mark Llewellyn, Channel Nine's head of news and current affairs. I had to make an appearance: Mark had been the first to approach me about joining *Today* and I was unsure how secure my position would become once he left the network. I kept looking around for a way to sneak out of the pub quietly.

Work get-togethers made me nervous; I always ended up blurting out some inappropriate comment, too loud, too political. My default position included plenty of nodding and smiling, trying to remain neutral to what was being discussed by my colleagues. Looking around the room at this farewell, I could see *60 Minutes* reporters Liz Hayes, Charles Wooley and my long-time 'girl crush' Jana Wendt. Soon Jana walked over to our group and I was immediately star struck. My throat went dry as she turned directly to me and said, 'You've been getting a lot of scrutiny, haven't you? Just hang in there.'

'I'll try,' I managed to reply.

'It's happened a lot to me over the years—you feel like the media attention couldn't get any worse and then it does for no real reason. But then it starts to bottom out and swing upwards in your favour, and there's no real reason why it does. You just have to ride it out.'

I appreciated Jana's advice and I couldn't quite believe my role model had words of wisdom just for me! I knew that working in the media could be tough and it wasn't a career for the faint-hearted. I also understood how brutal it could be for women. Commercial television is still primarily run by men, and some of them have very outdated, sexist views. I would like to say that it's changing and I suppose it is, but there have been numerous times during my career when I have been disadvantaged because of my gender. How can I forget the time when a boozy, domineering and terrifying news director pinned me against a hallway wall as he lurched back to work after his usual long, alcohol-fuelled lunch. He pressed his body against me but I managed to get away into one of the editing suites, where I rang one of the senior executives in tears. He counselled me and suggested that it wasn't a big deal; I got the distinct impression I should keep my mouth shut if I wanted to stay working in that newsroom.

Later in my career, after I had been reading the five o'clock evening news on the Ten Network for some years, I asked my boss if I could have an opportunity to read the main news story. I co-hosted with Ron Wilson, who read the first news story every night and also got to do all the live interviews. I figured I had paid my dues and it was reasonable to share the lead news story and the interviews each night.

'JC, have you got a minute?' I asked.

'Sure, lovey.'

'How about Ron and I alternate reading the main news story each night?'

'No.'

'No? Why not?'

'Because Ron's a man and you're a woman!'

Despite knowing deep down that that was the reason I hadn't been given the same opportunities as my male colleague, I was gobsmacked to have my boss articulate it so bluntly. I try to pick my battles but this was one I was prepared to fight. The next day I organised to have a meeting with the human resources department, who tried to fob me off by saying it was just my boss being his typical self, and of course that was not the reason.

'So what is the reason then?' I probed.

'Um, there is no reason. It's just the way it has always been done.'

'Well, it's time that changed then,' I persisted. 'If you look at the bulletins across the network, no female news presenter gets the chance to read the lead news story.'

'Really?'

By the end of the week I was finally given the chance to read the lead news story. The other female presenters around the network were now also 'permitted' to read the main news story on occasion. I had come a long way from the woman who'd be close to tears after being told the wrong pronunciations for difficult words and names by a male colleague. Thank goodness for the autocue operator, the person responsible for feeding the scripts through a device that would be projected onto the camera, who would yell out across the studio floor the correct way to say some of the trickier names. I wasn't going to give up my chosen career easily.

The closest I came to cracking during my *Today* experience was when I woke up one Sunday morning in 2006 to see more unpleasant headlines in both Sydney newspapers. The *Sunday Telegraph* TV guide included a cover photo after a poll voted me 'The Most Annoying Person on Television'. The *Sun-Herald* had an article entitled 'The Loneliest Job on TV', which went on to describe how increasingly isolated I had become in my position on *Today*. It was the final straw. Although neither article was the cruelest I had read, I felt at my lowest ebb.

What added to my anxiety was the campaign being run within Channel Nine. I was gobsmacked when I saw *A Current Affair* a few nights later and a story on how I was the most annoying person on television. I could usually laugh this kind of thing off, but it was all becoming too much. Peter rang his boss that night and ranted on my behalf, telling him that he was close to quitting. I told my loyal husband to calm down as we would need at least one pay cheque since I looked like losing my job at any moment!

My mood wasn't helped by the anxiety I had over the future of Milano, who was now six weeks young in my womb. While I flicked through the newspapers alone in bed, Peter once again on the other side of the world, I wondered whether it was all worth it. Yes, I could curl up under this doona all day and hide or I could get on with it. After wallowing for a few hours I realised I had to keep going. The worse it got, the more stubborn I became about it all not compromising my professionalism.

I kept setting the alarm and showing up on time to do my job. There was no way I was giving up; instead I chose to dig in my Dolce & Gabbana heels and be professional. Karl Stefanovic, one of my *Today* colleagues, also found himself targeted by the media during that time, and the pair of us would try and laugh it off. It was odd sharing a couch with my other co-hosts, three hours a day, five mornings a week, and have them say nothing about the situation. Their silence made me feel more isolated as there was a sense of everyone for themselves. It was not a team, and it was harder and harder to pretend to be a happy family on air. I'm still at a loss why no one said anything—perhaps it was simply because they wanted to keep their jobs and didn't want bad press about me to rub off on to them.

A few weeks later I was sitting on the couch in front of the television. *The 7.30 Report* had just finished, and I was making a few notes about the interview host Kerry O'Brien had completed with the foreign minister, Alexander Downer. I was going to be interviewing the minister the next morning so I wanted to make sure I was across the issues. It was getting close to bedtime so I was tempted to ignore my ringing mobile, but I thought I should answer it, just in case it was work.

It was Eddie. 'I tried to ring Peter to apologise, but I can't reach him . . .' I could hear the panic in his voice.

'What?'

'As a husband he would be furious . . .'

'What are you talking about?'

'You know, sorry for saying . . .'

'*What?*'

'But I didn't say it.'

'*What* didn't you say, Eddie?'

'I didn't say I was going to bone you.'

His explanation didn't help me. 'So why did you want to apologise to Peter if you didn't say it?'

'I've issued a statement to the papers saying I support you. Come in tomorrow after the show and we'll have a talk.'

I hung up the phone, sitting very still on the couch trying to fathom what Eddie had just told me. I had never heard the word 'bone' used in that sort of context before, but I didn't like the sound of it. I was angry but strangely calm, as if this phone call had landed me right into the centre of the perfect storm that had been hurling me around these past couple of months. Peter had just arrived home, and I called out to him from the living room.

'Eddie just rang,' I said.

'Really? He left a message on my mobile. What did he want?' asked Peter.

'He rang to say he wanted to apologise to you.'

'What?'

'For saying he was going to bone me . . .'

'Bone you—who the fuck says that?!'

'I feel sick,' I said.

A few minutes later my mobile rang. It was a journalist friend, who told me that Crikey, an online media website, had published a sworn affidavit made by my former boss Mark Llewellyn. Included in the document were details of a conversation about my future at the Nine Network. Peter and I tried to log on to the site but the story had already been taken down.

'I want to go in and talk to him, sort out what's going on,' Peter said furiously.

What *was* going on? I sensed something had just shifted in my universe, the planets had realigned in my favour. Kissing my darling Peter goodnight, I told him to wait and see what the morning would bring.

That night I fell into the deepest, most delightful sleep I'd had in many months. I slept well because I had a sense that my rock bottom had levelled out.

Someone called out to me as I reversed out of the garage early the following morning.

'Jessica, come on, give us a smile, I've been out here all night.'

I stopped the car and wound down the window to work out where the voice was coming from. It was still pitch-dark and I wanted to make sure I didn't run anyone over. A photographer appeared from behind the Moreton Bay fig next to our driveway, a cheeky grin on his face. He was rugged up against the cold, a red beanie on his head.

'Have you really been here all night?' I asked.

'Yep.'

I forced my biggest smile as his flash blinded me.

'See you,' I said, taking the handbrake off and reversing further onto the street before driving off into the darkness. I wasn't sure what was ahead but I knew it had already begun.

I hosted the *Today* show as usual that morning and later that day Channel Nine released this statement from Eddie McGuire: 'She has handled this with dignity and has shown a remarkable level of professionalism. She has my full support. We have confirmed with her that she remains as co-host of the show.'

That weekend a full transcript of what became known as the Llewellyn affidavit was published in every metropolitan newspaper. It became front page news after the Nine Network lost an injunction to stop media outlets from publishing its details. The document had been drawn up by my former boss Mark Llewellyn with his lawyer after he had been removed from his position as the head of news and current affairs at the Nine Network. In its twenty-six pages, Mark recounted a conversation that included the 'bone' reference. Here's the excerpt from the affidavit:

> At 3.30pm on 31 May 2006 I was called to a meeting with Eddie McGuire and Mr Jeffrey Browne, Executive Director at Nine. After some initial conversation about general news and current affairs topics a conversation took place as follows:

Mr McGuire said: 'What are we gonna do about Jessica? When should we bone her? I reckon it should be next week.'

By Jessica, McGuire was referring to Jessica Rowe, the presenter of the Today program.

I said: 'Are you sure you want to get rid of her?'

Mr Browne said: 'She's a laughing stock and if we keep her on air we will be the laughing stock.'

I said, 'Have you thought through what may happen if she goes? We went to all that trouble to get her from Ten and they copped bad publicity and now we'll cop it. Secondly, Peter Overton will be really upset and we run the risk of losing him from the network. That might be a real problem, because he might end up at Channel 7.'

In the wake of the affidavit being made public, I was overwhelmed by hundreds of emails, letters, notes, gifts and cards from viewers. The overnight *Today* producer started leaving a manila folder full of notes in my dressing room. Each morning, thanks to those generous words of support from people I had never met, I had the courage to keep smiling down the television camera.

The pendulum had started to swing the other way, just like Jana Wendt told me it would. The media coverage had also shifted; instead of focusing on me, it was now more about the management style at Nine. In just three weeks my bargaining power had risen exponentially, from no guarantee about my job security to public declarations of support from Eddie McGuire and Jeff Browne. All because of that four letter word.

As well, many women who I admired contacted me with words of encouragement. Among those marvellous women were Wendy Harmer, Tracy Grimshaw, Liz Hayes, Jana Wendt,

Tara Brown, Melissa Doyle, Paula Joye, Natasha Stott Despoja, Patrice Newell, Kerri-Anne Kennerley and Anne Summers. I had long admired Anne and was moved by the letter she sent me. Here is some of what she wrote:

> . . . I have some idea of what it is like to be under fire in a very public way and I know how horrible it is. Like me, you have a loving and supportive partner and I am sure he is a tower of strength, but I also remember how much I appreciated knowing that there were others out there—especially women—who were identifying with and supporting me. Please know that I am there for you. I am sure there are many others. Stay strong . . .

Apart from these fine women, there was also many wonderful men who made an effort to contact me. These blokes included US correspondent Robert Penfold, Seven News reporter Chris Reason, CNN's Hugh Riminton, Leigh Hatcher from Sky News and Channel Nine's Laurie Oakes. I kept the email that the late, great Peter Harvey sent me, summing up the situation in his unique style:

> Jess . . . the berber arabs of saudi arabia have a pretty cool saying. 'the dogs may bark but the caravan passes on' . . . which just about sums up the ill-informed drivel that people who criticise those of us in this business go on with. its just empty noise, signifying nothing . . . and we get on with life, with people who matter to us and whose opinion counts. so stuff'em Jess… the others don't matter, just dogs howling in the night. [sic]

Those good souls who reached out to me gave me the strength to keep facing down my detractors. It helped knowing that there were people in my corner. Although my job seemed more secure, what really kept me going was a far bigger prize, my darling Milano, who I hoped was stretching and somersaulting inside of me. Each crossed-off date in my diary brought me closer to my saving grace, the photo on the wall of the IVF clinic. It was getting harder to hide my swelling bosom and pot belly behind the stretchy patterned wrap dresses that I wore on camera each morning.

'You have a very photogenic baby,' said the sonographer.

There was our wish upon a star lying in a swirl of grey, waving her tiny arm around. The perfect little image made me laugh out loud. 'Hello there, my darling. We can't wait to meet you.'

Peter and I held hands tightly as we gazed at our baby. At last we had reached the twelve-week mark, and we were busting to reveal our secret cargo to the world. Many viewers had been my lifeline during those past eight months, so I decided to share the news with them first and surprise my workmates by announcing I was pregnant on the show on 21 July 2006.

The theme music began as we came back from a commercial break. 'You are watching *Today*,' I began, smiling widely at the camera. 'I have got something that I'd like to share with all of you. As many of you may know, the past couple of months have been a pretty tough and challenging time for me, but what has got me through has been the support of my husband, my family and friends, and also the support of so many of you. I can't thank you enough for all of the beautiful cards, letters and emails I've got from all of you.'

As I glanced around at co-hosts Karl, Richard Wilkins, Sharyn Ghidella and Cameron Williams, they looked shocked. I think they thought I was about to announce my resignation!

'Another thing that has got me through is a secret that I've had, and it's something I'd love to share with you all.'

'Tell us!' said Karl.

'I am three and a half months pregnant!'

'Get out!'

'Oh my god! Congratulations!' said Richard.

'Thank you, thank you,' I continued, still beaming. 'I'm due at the end of January. And I cannot tell you how excited and happy I am and Peter is. We have dreamt for such a long time about having a family, and finally our dream has come true.'

Later that week, Channel Nine launched its cricket coverage for the coming summer with a splashy party at Fox Studios. A Nine publicist met me at the door and walked me across the room to my front-row seat. I could sense the photographers and media writers watching me as we walked past Eddie, who was being interviewed by a journalist.

'Hey Jess, should we give them what they're waiting for?' said Eddie.

I glanced around, smiled and walked up to say hello. He gestured with his arms open, and I gave him an awkward kiss on the cheek.

A picture of the two of us laughing was on the front page of the papers the following day. Studying the image, I knew I should have just shaken Eddie's hand, but my nerves got the better of me. My whole life I had railed against being a nobody, not good enough. Although I was shy, I also wanted to stand out, perhaps believing that courting the spotlight would become a foil to my naturally reserved nature. Vanity, insecurity, ego and ambition had collided to give me the energy I needed to fight. Besides, I didn't want to look hesitant in front of the photographers; the show must go on.

And it did. Each morning I sat in my dressing room, reading my research notes while I ate muesli and held my blossoming belly. The next couple of months were the happiest of my time on *Today*. My rainbow-coloured wrap dresses expanded with me, and my heart expanded too when I felt the flutter of butterfly wings inside as my baby somersaulted and stretched her wings. I was humbled by the continued kindness of strangers, the hundreds of people who sent me cards, gifts, baby blankets, knitted cardigans and white-ribboned booties for my unborn baby. It was such a contrast to the hate mail I had received when I started at Nine. I had landed in a sweet patch, a snow dome of sunshine. Surely it couldn't stay this perfect for long?

I had decided to take four months' maternity leave. It seemed like a reasonable amount of time to have at home with a new baby before going back to work. A close friend, who was also a television presenter, was taking a similar amount of time away from her job. Naively I told friends that having a baby wouldn't change things much: she would fit around our lives, not become my life. My producer, who also didn't have children yet, suggested organising a crèche at work. Perfect, I thought, envisioning neatly expressing breast milk in my dressing room in between interviews with the prime minister, doing cooking demonstrations and chatting to the latest reality television stars.

Logically and calmly I explained to anyone who looked like asking that I would organise a 'night nanny' to care for the baby while I snuck out before dawn to work while Peter kept up his travelling commitments for *60 Minutes*. My sister, who already had a son and a second child on the way, sensibly stayed quiet. Mum also knew not to get into a debate with me about the practicalities of such an arrangement. My detailed plan of action tried to hide the sense of unease I still had about my job security. I needed to stay in control. There is a saying 'never take holidays when you work on television', because the person filling in for you will become your full-time replacement.

As I waved goodbye to viewers on my last show before going on maternity leave, with six weeks until I was due, I told them all that I would see them again soon. However, a part of me wasn't confident; my fill-in was the stunning supermodel Sarah Murdoch, who also happened to be married to Lachlan Murdoch. And as I drove past the security gatehouse at Channel Nine and waved at the guards after the show, I wondered if it would be for the last time.

CHAPTER SIX

Impatiently I snatched the immaculately wrapped present off the kitchen bench, putting it under my arm as I struggled to put down the plastic shopping bags full of pasta, Twisties, yoghurt and white chocolate. Peter and I were renting a holiday house on the South Coast, overlooking a beach with the whitest sands in the world. The present had been left by the owners, and I quickly pulled off the brightly coloured ribbon and ripped open the teddy bear–patterned paper.

'Look, Petee! It's a kids' book, ohhh and it's called *Guess How Much I Love You*,' I gushed.

'How thoughtful of those lovely people,' Peter said as he struggled to bring in my overfull bags of clothes, beach towels and bikinis from the car.

The book told of Big Nutbrown Hare and Little Nutbrown Hare's efforts to explain the love they have for each other. I conveniently ignored that it was a large male rabbit and his baby boy rabbit and decided to use female pronouns when I read the story out loud. I was still hoping for a little girl, although I kept that wish to myself. The book's catchphrase—'I love you right up to the moon and back'—was enough to have me crying happy tears when I read the book most mornings on the wooden balcony. Wearing only a pink polka-dotted bikini, I let the summer sun toast me and my swelling stomach. Purple stretch marks had spread across my bottom and the top of my thighs. These were my body's songlines and I celebrated the way it was expanding to make room for my baby. I couldn't take my eyes off my huge showgirl boobs! Becoming a C cup was very exciting for a girl who had struggled to fill a double A bra size for her adult life. My husband was also excited by my growing cleavage, but I had zero sex drive. So much for the articles he kept showing me, explaining how women had more interest in sex once they were pregnant.

Specks of bright white sunlight danced off the book's pages as I reached for another packet of Twisties. Before turning the page, I wiped my fingers on my red towel, careful to avoid getting orange stains on the story book. Milano, my 34-week baby, was doing full gymnastic routines in my tummy. Perhaps she was reaching out to the rays of sunshine or the sound of my voice as I read aloud, or maybe it was my bright orange breakfast that was getting her moving.

Sighing, I moved my legs and felt the buzzy adrenaline that had kept me alive this past year slowly start to seep out from my shoulders, tickling down to my fingers and toes. Getting up, I pulled a white cotton kaftan over my bikini before walking down the rough wooden steps that had been cut into the beach cliff. Jumping off the final step onto the beach, I smiled as I looked out to the waves breaking onto the rock pool. Just past the waves, some snorkellers kept disappearing from view as they dived down to check out the Port Jackson sharks hiding in the kelp. Walking along the beach was more my speed, each step I took on the powdery, squeaky sand shedding more of the tightness from my body. This coastline had been a constant in my life, a place I had come to as a teenager, a twenty-something upstart, a world-weary but naive single woman, a newlywed, a married woman heartbroken over IVF failures, and now here I was back again, pregnant. I looked behind and saw how the sun caught my damp footprints, leaving a silvery snail trail in my wake.

One lazy afternoon at the beach house my mobile rang, and I was surprised to hear Eddie McGuire's voice on the other end.

'Don't worry, we miss you!' he said jovially.

'Um, really?' I replied.

'I understand that feeling when you see someone else doing your job. It's going to be alright.' Only the day before there had been a newspaper article trumpeting the success of Sarah Murdoch in my role as co-host.

'Thanks for letting me know.' I said goodbye and hung up, touched and a little dazed by the call. Looking back, I wondered if he'd called because he knew he would soon be leaving his CEO role at the network. Or perhaps Eddie understood that being on television meant you had a fragile ego and needed reassurance.

We reluctantly left the beach house and headed back to Sydney as my due date got closer. Reality was rushing towards me: no longer would it just be Peter and me, soon there would be three of us. I spent most of January holed up in icy air-conditioned cinemas consuming films and choc tops. When I was not at the movies I was lying on our couch, feet up, flicking through crappy magazines. My hospital bag stayed next to the front door, packed with all the items that had been listed in my pregnancy bible, Robin Barker's book *Baby Love*. My sister Harriet, already a mum, also suggested I pack some large underpants for after the birth. Unsure why but too nervous to ask, I took her advice and packed ten pairs of size-sixteen black Bonds undies.

On 18 January 2007, shortly after midnight, I was woken by a growing pressure in my abdomen. This was it! Surprisingly though, I fell back asleep for a few hours. Around five o'clock in the morning I woke again.

'Peter, I'm having our baby!' I said, shaking him awake.

'What, *now*? Let's go!'

'Let's ring the hospital first,' I said.

A few minutes later I was through to the birthing unit at the Prince of Wales hospital. 'Hello, yes, my name is Jessica, Jessica Rowe, and I've gone into labour.'

'How far apart are your contractions?' asked the midwife at the other end of the line.

'I don't know, but my waters haven't broken yet.'

'Okay, we've got your details here. I'll get in touch with your doctor, but for now, time your contractions. Put a pad in, so you know when your waters have broken, and come in a few hours.'

'What do you mean "a few hours"?'

'About ten o'clock,' said the midwife.

My waters broke around eight in the morning and I got into the shower to distract myself. By then the contractions were coming strongly, the flicker and flutter of butterflies I had been feeling inside for months replaced by a pterodactyl, pushing and shoving to get out. I had to keep moving to cope with the growing pain. Each time I lay down a feeling of panic began to break over me. I had to get up to prepare myself for the wave of pressure that was crashing down onto my pelvic floor.

I paced around the house, all sorts of odd sounds coming out of my mouth as each contraction hit. 'Ah, ah, ah, ah, aaaaaaaah!' I was wearing down a path around the dining room table. Peter came close, trying to touch my shoulder, but I shrugged him away. My focus was becoming more inward as I concentrated on each contraction. It was still not ten o'clock but I couldn't wait any longer and told Peter to get me to the hospital.

Every speed bump, every turn, every stop at every goddamn red light hurt as the waves came closer and closer together. All I could focus on now was the voice of the commentator on the talkback radio station. '*Don't* turn that off!' I snapped at Peter. The short drive to the hospital had become the longest and bumpiest car trip of my life.

When we arrived at the hospital Peter and I were taken to a birthing suite and I put on a loose t-shirt. I had been fixated on what to wear and whether or not I was going to poo during labour. But I quickly discovered I didn't care what I wore and ended up naked pretty quickly. And there was far too much going on to think about the poo issue!

The doctor examined me and said I was already five centimetres dilated. Hooray! Only five centimetres to go. The midwife suggested I get into the bath, which was a wonderful idea, the warm water making me feel safely cocooned in a liquid world.

'I love you, I love you, I love you so much,' I said, holding my husband's hand as, in my delirious mind, we once again exchanged our wedding vows. Peter could not keep his hand still as he held mine, moving them up and down together. The crashing of the waves at Bondi Beach matched the crashes of pain that were rolling through my body. Suddenly the music of The Cure seeped into my head and I was dancing, spinning, flicking my long blonde hair on the dance floor at Reds nightclub in Rose Bay, my black and white midriff top showing off my smooth, tanned stomach. And then I suddenly became a mind reader: I knew what Peter was about to say, I knew what Megan, the midwife, would say. I had become the smartest person in the world, with the most incredible psychic ability! Through the haze I heard the midwife asking me if I needed to push.

'Yes, yes, *yes*, I do!' I exclaimed.

'Let's get you out of this bath then. It's time to have your baby.' Megan's words snapped me from my trippy moment. I was naked, strong—and stoned on happy gas.

Peter and Megan helped me onto the table. 'I'd like to have an epidural now,' I said.

'There's no time for that, you're about to have a baby!' the midwife laughed.

Time seemed to stop; there was no more gentle crashing of waves and mind reading, just work, hard work. It felt like it would never end. I would have a little rest between each contraction and then push down; the burning sensation was excruciating. All I could do was focus on the midwife's voice and listen to her instructions. The doctor arrived and told me he could see my baby's dark hair.

'I can see the head!' said Peter.

'Is there hair? What can you see?' I asked.

The midwife handed me a mirror. There it was, a damp patch of dark hair that belonged to my baby, my wish upon a star. I pushed and pushed and then I was told to stop pushing, but I couldn't resist the impulse as my pelvis stretched and expanded. The doctor pulled his tray of instruments closer and I kept glancing at where his hands were, hoping he was not going to reach for the scissors.

'Peter, put your fingers here,' said the doctor.

My husband carefully placed his long index fingers under the armpits of our baby and helped deliver her into the world. There was instant relief; the pain had stopped.

'It's a boy!' said Peter.

'Are you sure? It looks like a girl!' I said.

'Yes, it's a girl, a beautiful baby girl,' said the doctor as he rested our daughter on my chest. Relief poured through my exhausted body, and Peter and I began to cry, our happy, salty tears dropping onto our baby daughter's head. We were a family at last. I had never felt as close to my husband, or as in love.

Allegra gazed up at me, just thirty seconds old, lying on my breast and totally reliant on me for her survival. One of the great love affairs of my life had begun as she looked at me with one dark blue eye, her other eye gummed closed with vernix.

'Hello, my darling, there you are. I have waited so long to meet you. I love you, I love you, I love you.'

Things could only get better.

I had been conscientious in the hospital. I wanted to get a gold star for breastfeeding and made an effort to get to all the classes held in the maternity ward. Feeding was something I wanted to master—surely it would come naturally. Looking around at the other new mums crammed into the room, all their babies seemed to be happily sucking away. How could these women be smiling? Why weren't they wincing? Unlike me, none of them seemed to be breaking into a sweat. My pyjama pants were often damp, and it wasn't from my leaking vagina. I had a sanitary pad the size of a paddleboard wedged between my legs to soak up the copious amount of blood that kept flowing out of me, days after I had pushed my baby girl out; now I understood why my sister had suggested packing so many pairs of dark, comfy underpants. On top of this, sweat was pouring out of the skin at the top of my thighs, the dark, damp patches spreading across the front of my pyjama pants and clearly visible on the brightly coloured heart-print fabric. I think all the sweat was a by-product of the mixture of adrenaline and anxiety I had about breastfeeding.

I had expected some blood during labour, but I never knew nipples could bleed until now. Mine seemed to have been bleeding for days. Or was it nights? I had lost track of time burrowed away in the small hospital room with my new love. It felt safer to keep the curtains closed, shielded behind the drab hospital drapes. I wasn't ready to step out into this brand-new, scary, exhilarating world with my baby yet. Something terrible could happen to her. She might catch a cold. She might be woken from her long sleeps. Strangers might want to touch her cheeks and breathe on her. While Peter cheerily pushed Allegra out of the room and along the hospital corridors in her cot, I stayed on my bed. I could hear him chatting with the other new parents, but I didn't want to talk or even smile at them. All I wanted was to stay safely in my room, right at the end of the corridor.

But what I couldn't escape from was my bleeding nipples. I put cream on them, sat naked from the waist up in bed to give them 'plenty of fresh air', scrubbed them with a toothbrush to toughen them up. There was constant pain in my neck from looking down at my boobs. Was I holding Allegra the right way? Was her mouth open enough? Was she in the 'correct' feeding position? Well-meaning but rough midwives held my breast with one hand and hurled my tiny baby onto my nipple with the other. Surely I would be able to do this simple, natural thing. If I couldn't breastfeed my daughter, I had to be a bad mother. Your mind does strange things in the dead of night.

'I'm trying. I love you. Be patient with me. I love you. I love you. I love you. But please, little vampire, stop munching and crunching,' I whispered over and over again to my baby girl in the midnight hour.

My breasts had never had so much attention. I was used to being flat-chested, but now I felt like I had been visited by the plastic surgery fairy overnight. One morning I woke to find my breasts were hard, round, heavy and tender to touch. My black Bonds maternity bra was soon stuffed with cold cabbage leaves, the morning-shift nurse suggesting the leaves would take some of the pain away as my milk came in. It helped, but I smelt like a dirty fruit shop. I started to laugh and cry at the same time. I wasn't even home yet and already I felt adrift. No one told me it would be like this. I knew how to love, but I didn't know any of the practical stuff. I didn't know how to change my daughter's nappy (one of the confident, bossy midwives had suggested I could lose the gentle fairy taps and be more vigorous with the baby wipes at change time). I had never even held a baby properly before I had Allegra.

I had also bowed out of the bathing class given by the midwife dubbed 'the bath Nazi'. Her reputation for making new and not so new mothers cry because of their inappropriate bathing techniques was legendary; my girlfriends with toddlers had already warned me about her. Not surprisingly my husband, who can charm a cobra, passed her class with flying colours. 'She wasn't scary at all,' said Peter. 'She told me I was good at it.'

'Right, well bathing can be your job when we get home,' I told him. My head was already spinning with instructions on nappy changes, how to put a teeny-weeny singlet over an even teenier head, and the feeding—the feeding.

One night it was just too much and I buzzed the night nurse for some help. 'I don't know what I'm doing wrong,' I said, crying. 'My nipples won't stop bleeding.'

'Well, you certainly can't feed on them, and I don't know why you still are,' said the nurse.

'What do I do?' I said. 'One of the other nurses told me I could try feeding Allegra from a spoon.'

'Alright, but this will hurt,' said the nurse, reaching across and squeezing yellow colostrum out of my nipples. The drips of liquid gold were barely filling the teaspoon. How quickly you can feel just reduced to your body parts once you have a baby. Here I was, sitting with a woman I had met only moments before who was now squashing and tugging my nipples.

I was getting different advice from the myriad midwives that came into my room. I didn't know who had the 'right' advice and who I should listen to, so I kept trying to cram every new bit of information into my befuddled brain. My confidence ebbed away with each additional piece of conflicting advice. During one of my night-time research sessions I read the bizarre 'fact' that some women experienced something close to an orgasm when they breastfed their babies. What? Who was this hippy, trippy author kidding? Chrissie Amphlett's song 'Pleasure and Pain' kept playing on repeat in my sleep-deprived brain; I knew ecstasy was a long way off, but surely breastfeeding should not hurt so much. For me there was no fine line: I had fallen into a deep hole of pain, a whole new world that I didn't like at all.

A few hours later, after some snatches of sleep, I again inspected my nipples. My chin now seemed to be permanently attached to my clavicle due to the number of hours I spent examining my chest. My once pale pink nipples were still red and raw, despite feeding my daughter off a spoon overnight to give them a break. It was time to get some expert lactation advice. Surely that would help? My dear husband, who was spending every spare moment in the hospital with us, made sure he was also there for our appointment.

'Okay, let's see how you're feeding this baby,' said the lactation consultant.

I gritted my teeth, psyching myself up for the inevitable pain as Allegra latched on.

'Does it hurt?'

'I think so.'

'Well, if it hurts, you're not doing it properly.' She took my daughter roughly off my breast, and then shoved her back on my nipple.

'Does that hurt?'

'Umm, not really.' It did hurt, but I was too scared to say anything. I didn't want this woman manhandling my boobs again.

'You will have problems feeding because of your medical history with polycystic ovaries. Ask your husband to get these vitamins from the hospital chemist, okay? And this appointment costs three hundred dollars. I do take credit cards.'

Peter and I were shocked. There was nothing gentle or reassuring about her bedside manner. My husband silently handed over his credit card.

Allegra had some issues with her little right foot because it had become jammed up in my tummy. When she was born it was like she had a little flipper; essentially it would have meant she had a club foot if not for the wonders of modern medicine and physiotherapy. Allegra wore a tiny cast on her foot for the first few days of her life, which was replaced with a plastic splint that I had to wrap a tight bandage around to encourage her foot to start turning the right way.

I had managed to have some extra days in hospital with Allegra because of the extra physio she needed to do and the exercises I needed to learn. But it was now time to go home and I was terrified. How would I manage breastfeeding on my own? My nipples were still bleeding, it still hurt to breastfeed and I was worried that I wouldn't be able to feed my own baby and keep her alive. Peter and I couldn't even get Allegra into her car baby capsule on our own; the physio helped us adjust the straps and clip Allegra in securely. How would we manage at home? I sat in the back seat next to Allegra for the drive home. She had been constantly by my side in the hospital and I couldn't let her out of my sight. Peter kept looking at us both in the rear-vision mirror. I tried to smile at him through my tears. Tears of happiness, exhaustion and fear.

My husband shoved our heavy wooden gate open, leaning his tall body against it so our daughter and I could get past. Only seven days before we had left our little cottage as a couple; now we were returning as a family. I had hoped and prayed for this moment. I was finally a mother, and I had never felt so vulnerable. My heart, safely tucked away for so long, now felt like it existed outside of my body. A strong, spidery silver thread was linking it, tying me to this little soul, this six-day-old baby, who lay asleep in her capsule.

'Welcome home, my darling. This is the front door.' I sounded like a tour guide as I awkwardly lugged the capsule with my still sleeping baby girl around our cottage. 'This is the hallway, the kitchen, and here is your bedroom.' Allegra's eyes were still closed as I placed her and the capsule softly on the floorboards, late afternoon light filtering through the window.

'Petee, get your camera, we need to get a photo of this. Allegra in her bedroom.' I smiled at the camera, my eyes teary and arms aching as I carefully held the surprisingly heavy baby capsule. Nestled inside the lamb's wool liner my daughter slept on, oblivious to the importance of documenting this moment for her parents.

'What do we do now?' I asked.

'Um, should we just leave her in her room?' Peter suggested. Her bedroom had a brand-new white cot, white sheets on a pristine mattress, a fully stocked nappy change table and a white rocking chair.

'But if I leave Allegra sleeping, that could throw the routine out. I think I need to give her a feed again soon.' In one of my bags from the hospital I had a notebook documenting all the important stuff. It was full of dates, times, duration of breastfeeds, wet or dry nappy changes and what boob I had finished feeding on. One of the midwives had given me an information sheet explaining how often I needed to breastfeed Allegra. There was also the book *Baby Love*, and already I had dog-eared all of the pages in the breastfeeding chapter. Information had always been my saviour: if I had all the guidelines, facts, parameters and, research and jumped through the correct hoops, I would get the 'right' answer. But now I felt like no amount of information could help me work out if what I was doing was 'right'. Was it right to wake up my daughter? Should I give her a little poke so we could stay on track with the routine of feeds every ninety minutes?

'Why don't you have a sleep? I'm sure she's going to wake up soon,' Peter said.

'Alright, but get me the minute Allegra wakes up,' I said, before checking that we had plugged in the baby monitor correctly and switched it to full volume. But from my room I couldn't hear her snuffling sleep sounds, all I could hear was static and the sounds of cars passing outside. Exhaustion mixed with adrenaline meant I couldn't switch off and slow down my buzzing mind to get some sleep. Okay, I last fed on the left side and that was about two hours ago. When Allegra wakes up I need to start on my right—or was it my left? I need to find the right sort of cushion to rest her on when I feed. I need to make sure I sit in the right sort of chair with a straight back. What about my feet? I need a footstool, something to help my posture. I need to change her nappy before the feed—or do I do it afterwards? I need to make sure I have a bottle of water to drink constantly so I can keep up my milk supply. I need to . . .

'Mah, mah, mah,' came the sound from the monitor. I leapt up.

'My darling, my snuggle bunny, Mummy's here!' I rushed to her room and reached down to scoop her out of her capsule. She was funny looking, my baby girl, no chubby cheeks or angel curls. She reminded me of a little frog with long arms and legs that splayed everywhere, kicking off the white muslin wrap that I had clumsily tried to roll her up into before her sleep.

'Come on, darling, time for a feed,' I said, trying to sound confident. Who was I kidding? I was frightened.

Peter reassured me that it would be okay as I tried to get our daughter onto my breast. The front doorbell suddenly rang. We knew that it would be Chris, a mothercraft nurse who we had organised to come around and help. She came highly recommended through friends, who described her as a 'lifesaver' when they brought their babies home. I needed a lifesaver! Chris first met with Peter and me while I was still pregnant and had helped me organise the nursery; she'd also had some suggestions about how I could manage returning to work. She would be coming over regularly to help once Allegra was born.

'Stop, stop feeding now,' said Chris. 'You can't feed on those breasts. They're bleeding.'

I started to sob with relief. 'I tried.'

'Of course you did, it's not your fault. The hospital should have stopped you feeding once they saw the state of your nipples.'

'I'm so glad you're here,' I said, as Chris gently took Allegra from me and asked me to tell her everything.

'I can't feed. I don't know what to do. It hurts, it's bleeding. I can't feed my baby.'

'Oh yes, yes you can,' she said. 'We just need to get those nipples better before you give it another go. I'm going to write a list of supplies that Peter can get from the chemist.'

My ever-dependable husband was dispatched to the all-night chemist and returned in record time with bottles, nipple shields, dummies and formula. I already had a steriliser and a breast pump and now even more instructions to write down in my notebook: when to pump, when to sterilise, how to freeze breast milk and when to use formula. Now I really felt like a failure. I was the world's worst mother because my baby was going to be fed formula—I was lowering her IQ, making her obese and setting her up for a lifetime of delinquency. But Chris reassured me and wrote down everything that I needed to get through the evening. She gave me a hug and said she would be back the next morning. I was relieved to have a written plan. Perhaps if I just focused on the notes for the night it would be okay.

Peter and I didn't sleep much that evening as we took turns to check that Allegra was still breathing. I put my ear as close as possible to her nose to listen for her gentle pixie breaths. After a while we took her out of the cot and put her in the fresh, spotless pram right next to our bed. Still our peaceful girl didn't stir, she just kept sleeping. I pulled the pram even closer to my side of the bed. I missed the feeling of her somersaulting and stretching inside of my tummy. I wanted to keep her safe. Always.

Amber and pastel pink light was breaking apart the dark night sky. I leant into Peter as we looked out our back kitchen window, watching the sunrise and listening to the sound of rainbow lorikeets calling to each other in the wattle tree near our fence as they started their day. Peter was wearing his faded orange t-shirt that was ripped around the neck and sleeves, a favourite item of clothing that I had banned him from wearing outside the house. I buried my head into his shoulder and inhaled; he smelt safe and secure—oh how I loved that about him. I breathed out, but only a little. We had survived our first night as a threesome. My mobile beeped with a message from a girlfriend: *You made it. You got through the night.* I wondered what she was doing awake. Her boys were in primary school—surely you wouldn't choose to be up at this time?

The hum of the steriliser, cleaning its bottles and dummies, was competing with the sound of static coming through on the baby monitor. Despite keeping the volume turned right up, still all I could hear was the noise from the street. A garbage truck pulled up out the front and I could hear the smash of glass as it was tipped into the back. Next to the noisy monitor, the kitchen bench top was covered with items that I barely knew existed a week before: a breast pump, nipple shields, cherry-shaped dummies and tins of formula. The explosion of bottles was jarring to my ears, my senses on high alert. Allegra slept on. Should I wake her up? Did she need another feed?

'I'm sure you should never wake a sleeping baby,' said Peter.

'Who told you that?'

'I don't remember.'

'But I have to make sure Allegra is getting enough milk. I have to keep feeding her, so my body can keep making more milk.' I was sure Chris had told me to wake Allegra for her morning feed.

I went into our bedroom to give Allegra a little nudge in her pram. I told myself I wasn't really waking her up, and if she didn't open her eyes straight away I would creep out. Her little hand had wriggled free from her wrap. As I stroked those tiny fingers I could hear her breathing change. I touched her delicate cheek and leant closer to inhale her soft, sweet new smell. Her almost translucent eyelids flickered open, reluctantly waking up from her watery dreams. Allegra's dark blue eyes gazed into mine, and the simple trust I saw there opened a window on my soul. The crushing feeling of love and responsibility threatened to overwhelm me as I teetered on the cusp of a new life. Nothing would ever be the same again.

'What's wrong?' asked Peter.

'Nothing, this insurance ad is making me cry.' My emotions felt raw and exposed, and I seemed to be constantly on the verge of tears. And this father saying goodbye to his little baby in the television commercial when he went off to work was making it worse. I had always been a sensitive soul, but this was the first time a TV ad had made me cry! The midwives at the hospital had told me that it was natural to experience 'the baby blues' a few days after giving birth, describing it as being teary and emotional over pretty much anything and everything. My sister Harriet, who had just had her second child, also told me she always felt more emotional just after she had her babies. She said it was normal to feel that way—but was it normal to feel undone by the simple mechanics of assembling a pram? I had interviewed prime ministers and pop stars and dealt with Machiavellian bosses, but apparently I couldn't cope with a pram. It seemed impossible to unclip the blue bassinet and collapse the wheels properly so I could fit the damned designer buggy into the boot of my car.

The twenty steep stairs leading from the door to our front gate had left me feeling trapped at home. After slipping down them once when pregnant I was tentative whenever I went up or down, but now my anxiety had increased because I had to get Allegra and her pram up those steps to reach the street. The only way I could get out of the house was if Harriet came over and helped me lift the pram, with Allegra sleeping in it, up the stairs. Then we would walk the streets of the neighbourhood, pushing our babies in their prams. Her little boy, Elliot, was just a few months older than Allegra, and the pair of them slept while we talked and walked. Harriet was gently reassuring, offering suggestions and tips about breastfeeding. It was good to leave the walls of the house behind and feel a part of the world again. I had always been close to my sisters but having Allegra had brought me even closer to Harriet.

She understood my vulnerability, and our walks and talks together were a godsend for me.

Life seemed to return to normal quickly for my husband. Of course he was changed because he was now a father, but he was able to leave the house, drive his car, get dressed, have a shower and walk out the door alone! He was already back at work when Allegra was just three days old, his parental leave cut short because he was 'needed' to do a story for *60 Minutes*. Not much had changed for him, but everything had changed for me. I didn't want to be resentful but I was. It was hard to have a shower and get out of my pyjamas. I didn't have the physical or emotional energy to get changed. Every moment was consumed with thinking about Allegra and what I needed to do for her. I didn't want to leave our daughter alone for even a moment while I got into the shower. There was so much to do and my needs came last. I didn't care about myself anymore, all that mattered was our baby girl. My body no longer felt like my own: it was a feeding, bleeding machine. Even with years of early morning starts for work, I had never experienced tiredness like this where life was broken down into three-hour feeding blocks. Days and nights blurred into one, and there was no off switch. I always needed to be on and ready to feed, change, snuggle, wrap or try to settle Allegra. I tried to snatch pockets of sleep while my baby slept, but even then my dreams were full of sterilising bottles and singing lullabies.

I adored my baby girl, but I felt exhausted and strung out from the relentless routine. Breastfeeding wasn't getting any easier; my nipples were still bleeding, and even though Allegra was getting formula as well as my breast milk she wasn't putting on enough weight. It felt like another black mark against my name every time her weight didn't match up with the appropriate gain on the chart from the baby clinic. And was it normal to end up in tears when I couldn't clip Allegra and her baby capsule into the car? Getting out of my pyjamas and out the door with my new baby felt like such an achievement.

'What have you done to Allegra's car seat?' I screamed at Peter down the phone.

'Nothing. I haven't touched it since I got Allegra out of the car yesterday.'

'You've broken it, you must have. It's not working. I can't do it. And I have to get to the mothers' group meeting!'

Allegra blinked up at me.

'Okay, let's try it again,' Peter said patiently. 'Angle the front of the capsule into the clip. Once you hear it click then push the back of it down.'

'It's not working!'

'Check the front seat, maybe you pushed it back by mistake.'

'No, I wouldn't have done that.'

Putting Allegra down on the footpath in her capsule, I pulled the seat forward.

'Oh, um, I must have done that yesterday. It's working now. Love you,' I said, ending the phone call.

'Mummy is silly. Sorry about that, my darling. Let's go and meet some more mummies and babies.'

I was the last to arrive at the baby clinic. Struggling to push open the door, I tried to balance Allegra in her baby capsule on one arm and lug a huge bag on the other, crammed full of wipes, dummies, disposable nappies, a leopard-print change mat, spare clothes for Allegra and breast pads. I sighed noisily as I came in, glancing at the other mothers in the group. None of them looked flustered or sweaty, and I bet they had no problems getting their baby capsules into the car. They were sitting in a circle, blissfully breastfeeding and snuggling their babies. I found the last chair in the circle at the back of the room and placed Allegra at my feet in her capsule, happily sucking on her pink dummy.

'You're not using that, are you?' said the nurse running the group.

'Yes, it's helping me with settling Allegra. And she really likes it.'

'No, no, that's no good. She won't be able to latch on properly for feeding. You can't rely on that.'

I looked around the group of women, holding back my tears. A few of their babies had dummies as well. Surely it wasn't that bad?

'Isn't this the best thing you've ever done?' said one mother.

'It just gets better and better,' replied another.

Christ. Next I'll hear that they orgasm while breastfeeding.

'Oh, and I just love breastfeeding.'

I stayed silent. No, this is not the best thing I have ever done, I thought, it is the worst thing I have ever done. I don't know what I am doing. I love my baby girl, but it's excruciatingly painful to breastfeed. I can't collapse the pram. I am using dummies, formula and bottles. And it's not getting better, it's getting worse. I can't sleep, even though I have never been so dog-tired in my life. I feel out of control, scared and overwhelmed. And I shouldn't be feeling like this. I have wanted to have this glorious, golden baby for such a long time. It was such a struggle to have her. It should be the happiest time of my life and I should be grateful. I had always promised that I would never be one of those mothers who complained. All the women there looked calm and capable—not like me. But I kept my chirpy veneer in place, nodded my head and smiled. I would not be coming back to this meeting.

I had never been more alone. Somehow I had fantasised that I would find my tribe at this meeting. Surely I was not the only mother who was struggling? What was wrong with me? I was too scared to open up in front of these women, who seemed to wear their motherhood like a badge of honour, a competition that they were winning. I had always been so in control of my life and believed that by working hard at something it would turn out the right way. But I had never worked harder at anything and been so powerless of the outcome. I was not winning this mothering caper. And I couldn't tell anyone.

CHAPTER SEVEN

Mum's bedroom was right next to mine, the walls not thick enough to muffle the cries that got louder and louder. Frightened, I would creep out of my single bed and walk to her closed bedroom door, sliding my back down it to sit on the floor, still and quiet. Frozen in that position, I was torn between opening the door to comfort her and sneaking back to bed. But each night I couldn't move from that spot until the terrifying sounds on the other side of the door had stopped; only then would I go back to my bed and sleep. I never asked her about those noises in the night. The smiling, happy mother I knew in the waking hours was so different to the woman I heard behind her closed door once the stars had come out to brighten the night sky. I was an eight-year-old, obsessed with ballet and chocolate Monte biscuits, but already I'd learnt about putting on a brave face.

Mum was finally diagnosed with bipolar disorder when I was about ten years old. Thankfully it's an episodic illness, so there are plenty of times when she is well. But there have been many times when she has fallen into the dark hole of severe depression. Mum has spent months at a time in psychiatric wards, taken numerous medications, and endured endless bouts of electroconvulsive therapy to try to shock her brain out of that terrible place in which she has battled to survive. Throughout my teenage years, Mum was hospitalised at least every twelve months. I had become expert at looking for the warning signs, Mum's face becoming drawn and the dark rings under her eyes more pronounced as she existed on almost no sleep.

My sisters and I would be woken by the sound of the vacuum cleaner in the middle of the night as Mum's illness made it hard for her to sleep. I would spy Mum dressed only in her singlet and underpants, vacuuming the bookshelves. Other times we would wake and find twenty homemade hairclips that Mum had painstakingly sewed with fake flowers and pretty blue velvet ribbon during the night. Once we came home from school to find a whole new lounge in the living room; that was quite a surprise as Mum didn't have a lot of spare money to be splashing out on new furniture. The next day she bought five straw sunhats, identical apart from their colours. She said she couldn't decide which one she liked best. My sisters and I didn't realise at the time but this behaviour meant Mum was in the manic phase of her bipolar illness. She would be full of extreme ideas, have extraordinary energy and not want to go to sleep. Her mind was operating on fast forward. Soon after this sort of exuberance, Mum's mood would inevitably darken. She would snap at our chatter, telling us we were too noisy. But I couldn't stop trying to make her laugh or smile. I was on alert, ready with my repertoire of funny stories.

The doctors were trying to work out the best medication to keep her stable as she couldn't tolerate the standard lithium treatment that worked well for many bipolar sufferers. I remember coming home from high school one afternoon and asking Mum how she had spent the day.

'Looking at the walls.'

'Oh . . . You won't believe what happened at school today. I was swinging on my chair during Latin and then the—'

'Please stop, you're too loud.'

'Can I get you a cup of tea? What about I go down to Woolies and buy you a scorched peanut bar? You know, your favourite?'

'Be quiet, please . . .'

With that I walked out of the living room back into the kitchen where my sisters sat around the old rectangular pine table. Harriet had already set out three glasses, so I got the milk out of the fridge and asked Claudia to reach the Milo in the cupboard. Right, today I would put three tablespoons of Milo into each of our cups. Usually we weren't allowed to have that much, but right now I was in charge.

When Mum started to spiral downwards she was increasingly impatient with the normal bustle of family life, becoming snappy and then angry with us. One day she yelled through the front door at me when I had left my keys at home. She threw the keys down the stairs at me and crawled back to the living room, unable to walk as the drugs she had been prescribed were reacting very badly with her system. But my sisters and I were unaware that it was the medication that caused such terrible changes to her mood.

I became even more frightened when Mum's impatience was replaced with a sinister quiet. This had been the pattern of her illness, first the mania, then the irritation and now the stone statue. Sitting in her specially upholstered blue chair, she appeared frozen as she stared at the new couch and dirty cream wall. My sisters and I would leave her there in the mornings after trying to tempt her with a cup of tea and Vegemite toast. When we returned in the afternoon Mum would be sitting in the same spot, barely registering when I kissed her soft cheek, her tea cold and the toast untouched on the coffee table. It was like our mum was no longer there, just a shell. When she was like this we knew it was time for her to go to hospital, and thankfully she didn't need much convincing that was the safest place for her.

I remember on one occasion, sitting on the edge of her hospital bed, I first set myself the task of trying to get her to smile. Just a hint of a smile would be enough; I wanted to see some light and sparkle return to her beautiful green eyes. Instead all I saw was my mother hunched on the corner of her bed staring vacantly at me. The sweet smell of the yellow jonquils I was clutching seemed to wilt when faced with the sadness and desperation hanging in this grim, grey room. There was no place for yellow spring flowers here. How could my naive songs, stories and jokes compete with such choking despair? But still I kept trying to pull her out of despair; that was my job, my role as Miss Cheerful.

I've had a lifetime of rehearsals for putting on a brave face. It is a gift I developed from a young age, and my self-cast role became perfect training for a career in front of the camera, where it's important to be consistent, calm and cheerful regardless of whatever else is happening in your life. It's a tendency that I still find hard to shrug off, especially when I need to ask for help. So it seemed a sign of weakness for me to admit I was struggling as a new mum when I was supposed to be happy. I had seen what had happened to my mother when it was all too much, and certainly some part of me was fearful that I too might end up in a psychiatric ward. My mind was making all sorts of catastrophic leaps and I was terrified about where it would end. Would my life also unravel? Would the despair inside of me leach out and become those same dark, dead of night sobs hidden on the other side of the bedroom door while my baby and husband were locked out, listening on the other side?

From the outside, in the sunny light of day, I at long last had my baby. My family was complete, so what reason did I have to feel anxious, insecure, out of my depth and unhappy? I had everything, but I was struggling. I wanted to be capable and strong, to be everything to my daughter that I felt my mother couldn't always be because of her illness. I didn't realise how high I was setting the bar or how much pressure I was putting on myself. Up until then I had managed to crash through and keep going through the sheer force of my cheery personality.

But the skill set and default mechanism that had got me through my 36 years was not working anymore. What I really needed to do was ask for help, but instead I kept up my award-winning performance as the perfect mother with the perfect baby. Chris, the mothercraft nurse, would call me each morning to talk through how the night had gone. I listened dutifully to her suggestions about the day's routine, wrote them down and did my best to make it work. Then I'd put on my pink leopard-print sundress with matching pink ballet flats and my big black Jackie O sunglasses to hide my tired, frightened eyes from the world. It looked beautiful from the outside, but inside I felt ugly, unworthy and a failure.

I couldn't stop looking at Allegra as I tried to manoeuvre the orange pram over the giant tree roots. The Moreton Bay fig outside our house has a magnificent sturdy trunk and glossy, green leaves, but the pram's back wheels kept getting stuck on its unwieldy roots. The safety strap from the pram was wrapped tightly around my wrist as I shoved hard to get it moving along the concrete pavement. I was sure I detected a smile from my baby girl as she looked up at her sweaty mother. Yes, it was a smile, her first smile, even if my aunt would later tell me it was just wind. Was that a dimple I could see in her cheek? I was sure it was. You're just too good to be true, my beautiful baby girl. The pair of us made slow progress along the street.

'How are you?' my neighbour asked, as she was walking back from the supermarket with her arms full of shopping bags.

'Great, just great,' I replied with a large smile, not wanting to stop for a chat. Allegra was starting to doze off thanks to the rocky rhythm of the wheels bumping along the footpath and I didn't want anything to interrupt her morning sleep as we walked down the street to pick up milk, bread and my morning coffee.

'When are you going back to work?'

'Soon.'

It was odd. I was always being asked the question about when I was heading back to my job. The work question had now replaced the 'When are you getting engaged/married/having a baby?' questions. Unfortunately, I didn't brush off this latest inquiry as polite conversation but instead used it to put more pressure on myself. When *was* I going back to work? Back to my life?

I had grown up in a generation of young women who had been taught that we could have it all, and that we deserved it all, too. As a feminist, it was part of my belief system that my gender was not going to hold me back from achieving the work-life balance that I had naively predicted would accompany motherhood. I would be a superwoman, a supermum who could take it all in her glittering caped stride.

But now that I was a mother, I was forever changed. I didn't realise the exquisite, delicious hold my daughter would have over me. The leave form I had filled out while my baby was tucked safely inside me requested four months' maternity leave. Sixteen weeks away from work sounded fine to me then; it would show my bosses I was very, very serious about returning to my job on *Today*. However, that arbitrary number had little relevance now that my Allegra had weaved her spell over me. I wasn't ready for her to be looked after by someone else so I could face a television studio again. Despite feeling adrift and lonely, it was impossible to imagine being apart from my daughter. I wanted her, needed her to be close to me all the time. The love I had for her was suffocating and all encompassing. She was too precious for me to leave in the care of just her father or her grandparents. It didn't matter that my dear father-in-law was an eminent paediatrician who had a lifetime of experience looking after babies and children. I was the only one who believed I could care for Allegra properly!

My mobile phone was ringing; eventually I found it right at the bottom of my bag under baby wipes and change mat, but I was tempted to ignore it when I recognised the number on the caller ID. It was work, and I didn't want to be talking about anything other than my brand new baby.

Allegra was less than two weeks old, so I knew without a doubt that I wasn't ready to leave my baby yet. But would I ever be ready? Despite having taken four months' maternity leave, which Nine had signed off on, I suspected there was a strong chance I would not get my television job back if I didn't return to work soon.

I wanted to be left in peace for a little longer before having a conversation about returning to television; I wasn't ready to be thrust back into the pressure of work.

After working in television for more than fifteen years, I understood it was a cut-throat environment. And sure, many people work in cut-throat environments, but what made working in the media especially brutal was how it was all played out so publicly. In his 1988 book *Generation of Swine*, Hunter S Thompson aptly describes the TV business as a 'cruel and shallow money trench through the heart of the journalism industry, a long plastic hallway where thieves and pimps run free and good men die like dogs, for no good reason'.

It also didn't have a good track record of supporting working mothers. At the time there were few senior women in television who had children. I had spoken with Melissa Doyle, who had returned to full-time work hosting *Sunrise* soon after having her second baby, to see how she did it. I had known Melissa for many years, and she was supportive but honest that some days were harder than others to make it work. So I *could* make it work, couldn't I? And I knew of working mothers in other professions who seemed to juggle it all.

Breastfeeding was still a struggle. My stubborn nature meant I wasn't going to give up just yet even though my nipples were still bleeding and sore. I also got mastitis because I kept feeding on my damaged nipples. Chris, the midwife, was still visiting and phoning regularly to check on how we were coping with the breast- and bottle-feeding. Allegra was getting topped up with more and more formula to keep her weight up. She was getting most of her nourishment from the formula so I don't know why

I was so obsessed with still being able to breastfeed. My mum kept encouraging me to just bottle feed Allegra.

'Darling, I bottle fed you and you turned out just fine. Please stop putting yourself through this.'

Allegra was now just over two and half months old and I knew that it would be easier to have her bottle fed for when I went back to work. But it was getting harder to think clearly in my exhausted, sleep deprived state. I still wanted to have time to enjoy my maternity leave before work came crashing back into my fragile new world. Peter and I had talked about extending my leave but I still wasn't sure if this was a good idea. My dear, constant husband told me he would support whatever decision I made and that he would make it work, for me and for our family.

My confidence plunged further when I opened the newspapers about ten days later. Allegra was wrapped up in her cot having her morning sleep while I sat on our shabby beige linen couch, the baby monitor and a pile of newspapers on the coffee table in front of me. The white shutters on the living room windows were letting in soft yellow morning light. My cat, Audrey, who I had pretty much ignored since we brought Allegra home, was rubbing herself against my legs, desperate for some attention. Auds managed to get a quick pat before I hauled myself off the couch to walk down our back steps and put on yet another load of washing, a bluc laundry basket full of white jumpsuits, miniature singlets and pink muslin wraps balanced between my arms. There was a clean load of washing to be pulled out of the machine first though; a magpie warbled as I pegged doll-sized clothes on the line.

One of the tips in my baby book suggested resting whenever the baby slept, so I went back to lie on the couch with the newspapers. I flicked through the papers in an attempt to feel vaguely in touch with the news. I was halfway through Sydney's *Daily Telegraph* when my heart dropped on spotting an article that read: 'This time, Nine's director of news and current affairs Garry Linnell has agreed that Rowe—currently on maternity leave—could be the "fly in the ointment" if ratings dip on her return.'

I felt sick and angry. I should have thrown the newspaper in the bin, but I had to keep reading: 'The first-time mother has also reportedly struggled to settle her 12-week-old daughter Allegra, making her decision to leave the child more difficult.'

Nameless sources were now questioning my mothering ability—how dare they! I had told absolutely no one about my worries and fears for my daughter. I wanted to be the best mother I could be; I also wanted to be the best I could be at my job. But I needed to have a break, time to catch my breath. And I had to get this breastfeeding thing right.

Two days later, the network rang to tell me that I no longer had a job on the *Today* show. People who know me well understand I'm not the cussing sort of girl, but the language I let fly after that phone call was enough to make a truckie blush. Just as well the only person who heard me unleash the most extreme of expletives was the cat, Alfie. He might have been hiding under his paws at the time. I screamed through the house. Thankfully Allegra snoozed on through my rage, dreaming of a kinder world, asleep in her cot, blissfully unaware of what her mother was unleashing in the living room. Hell hath no fury like a new mother who has lost her job. Deep down I knew I didn't have the mongrel energy to fight back. I just wanted some peace and uninterrupted time with my new love.

While Allegra kept sleeping my head whirred with a peculiar mixture of rage and relief. I had known this would happen but I knew I could now *stay* with my baby.

Although I was exhausted, I barely slept that night. When the alarm went off at five o'clock, I got up in the darkness and dressed carefully for the morning ahead in a white silk shirt and black suit, squeezing my feet into my favourite peep-toe heels for the first time in weeks. I had organised for one of the midwives from the hospital to come and babysit Allegra. My mind was racing. There were two ice cube trays of frozen breast milk in the freezer and I had sterilised ten bottles and five pink dummies. I didn't want to leave Allegra with a babysitter but Peter insisted he would take me into the meeting with my lawyer, wait for me and drive me home afterwards. The diamond strap over my toe winked up at me as Peter and I walked out the front door together. I looked back to see Allegra happily nestled in the arms of the midwife.

The morning sun was just starting to light up the harbour as I waited for my solicitor to arrive in the travertine marble-floored reception area. I kept gazing out through the massive glass windows at the Sydney Harbour Bridge and kept my hands firmly on top of my black pants to stop my fingers shaking with anger and exhaustion. Strung out on adrenaline, my heart was racing and, despite the cool air conditioning, patches of sweat formed under my arms.

But I left the first meeting eager to get home to Allegra, my head whirring with thoughts of legal statements and my professional life. Again, I didn't sleep much that night. I'd already learnt that in life I had to pick my battles and I realised I didn't have the stamina for this one. I was fragile and needed to focus on my baby girl and family.

As part of the ultimate settlement nutted out over long and stressful meetings with Channel Nine and its lawyers, I agreed not to discuss the final terms or even the details of the negotiations.

After the final meeting, I arrived home, so exhausted I dropped down onto our front lawn in my suit and began to sob. I didn't want to get up—I *couldn't* get up as my world was spiralling, spinning and crashing down around me. Harriet slipped off my high heels and held my hand while Mum stroked my hair. My tears fell onto the soft green grass and the smell of dirt filled my nostrils. The make-up I had so carefully applied bled down my face in a black, streaky mess. And still my precious baby slept, wrapped snugly in her cot, oblivious to the despair of her mother.

Who was I now that I didn't have a title, a job description? I was a failure, a joke, a laughing stock. My shooting star had crashed and burnt, proving all the naysayers right. I was a fraud and a fake and I had been unmasked. Now I was just a mother, and not a very good one. I wanted to be the perfect mother and the successful career woman who wouldn't take any nonsense from men. But I couldn't even breastfeed properly, my baby wasn't putting on weight, and I had lost my job.

CHAPTER EIGHT

I struggled to haul Allegra up to our front gate in her baby capsule, balancing the awkward carrier without losing my footing on the wretchedly steep stairs. Allegra and I were meeting Harriet and her family for Sunday breakfast after waking to the front-page news in the papers about my sacking from *Today*. The press release had been leaked a day early. It was three brief sentences, including a statement that 'Jessica Rowe would not be returning to the Network and that Nine and Jessica had reached an agreement that would allow Jessica to take up other opportunities for her career'. Peter was away in Melbourne for television's so-called 'night of nights' to present an award at the Logies. What a difference a year makes; only twelve months earlier I had been hosting the red-carpet coverage of the awards, with my darling Allegra, no bigger than a fingernail, secretly keeping me company.

At the top of the stairs, I suddenly noticed the stretched shadows of many pairs of shoes slipping under the cracks of our front fence. Shoving my knee into the gate, I opened it to find myself and Allegra surrounded by journalists, bright artificial lights, TV cameras and photographers.

'Jessica, how are you? Anything you would like to say?'

'Jessica!'

'Jessica?'

'I'm feeling good, it's a beautiful day,' I grimaced, desperate to shield Allegra from the flashes.

The wretched baby carrier was letting me down again. I had opened the back door of the car but could not clip Allegra and her capsule into the seat. The frozen smile on my face was making my cheeks ache, while the panic kept rising inside me. I wanted to flee. I wanted to keep my baby girl safe, away from this scrutiny.

'What will you do?

'I just want to get my daughter into her car seat.'

My hands finally stopped shaking enough to clip Allegra in. Taking deep breaths, I walked around to the driver's side and fumbled my key into the ignition. Breathe, breathe, I said to myself, looking into the rear-vision mirror and slowly reversing out into the street. How I wanted to put my foot on the accelerator, turn the wheel sharply and run down the media crews! My baby girl had been exposed to their bright lights, flashes and oversized camera lenses. Just breathe, breathe. Once I was out of the street, I stopped and, crying, turned around to my baby girl to stroke her head.

'My darling, I'm sorry. I am so sorry, my darling girl. Mummy is so sorry,' I whispered again and again.

Despite my permanent sleep haze, I managed to put on my happy mask each time I was out of the house. Harriet and I walked side by side, pushing our sleeping babies in their prams. The air on my face felt good; perhaps I was just imagining the pane of glass between me and the world. The sun toasted my back as I struggled with the cover of Allegra's pram to protect her from the harsh morning light. As I clipped the sun protector to the top of the pram's canopy, I noticed the tiny purple birthmark on her eyelid was beginning to fade. Both of her eyelids started flickering and I wondered what my baby girl was dreaming of today. Her eyes stayed closed as the rhythm of the pram's wheels on the footpath lulled her back to sleep.

'How are you going with the breastfeeding?' I asked my sister.

'No problems,' said Harriet.

'So it doesn't hurt? I don't know what I'm doing wrong. I can't do it.'

'It's okay—it used to hurt me, but just keep going.'

I didn't want to keep going. Although I was tempted to open up to Harriet about my fears, I wasn't ready to admit them to myself. If they just stayed in my head perhaps they would disappear. Putting voice to my anxieties might make them become all too real and I didn't know how I would manage that. Adrift, my mind started to stray further and further from the reality and routine of my day. And the days were never-ending; the time between dusk and dawn and dawn and dusk seemed endless. I stumbled through, dividing my day into two- and three-hourly feeding slots as well as changing, snuggling and settling Allegra back to sleep. It all blurred into one big mess of exhaustion. I fantasised about going to bed like Sleeping Beauty and not waking up for a long, long time. How much sleep I was getting, or not getting, became an obsession.

Was anyone getting enough sleep? I was ready to slap mothers who told me their baby breastfed easily and quickly then slept deeply all night. Who were they kidding? Or perhaps I really was the odd one out.

I isolated myself even further. True to my word, I didn't go back to that mothers' group, and I cancelled my appointments with the community nurse who had been running that group because she chastised me for using a dummy for Allegra. The only thing I kept doing was walking the streets with my sister Harriet, somehow thinking this would keep me connected with the outside world and I could walk my way through the fear, pretence and anxiety. Some days, when the sunlight warmed my face and brought colour to my cheeks, I believed I had managed to keep the vampires from the door. I grabbed those moments, hoping they would lengthen into an hour or two. But once I closed the front door, no light came through. I was stuck, trapped, observing the world without me taking part in it.

Although I worried that Allegra wasn't putting on enough weight, I kept up the pretence of breastfeeding. The midwives at the hospital had told me that breast milk was best, and I had to give my baby the best possible start in life. I was still obsessed with getting my daughter to breastfeed properly. But even before I tried to get Allegra onto my breast she would start screaming; the scent of anxiety, despair and desperation must have been oozing out of me. Come on, come on, why won't you just open your birdlike mouth and let me feed you?

The worst was when friends came to visit and I sat on the couch opposite them trying to breastfeed. My stomach and chest felt tight and my throat would start to close up until I couldn't swallow properly. I felt naked, exposed, and it was getting harder and harder to keep up my daylight performance. When the phone rang I didn't want to pick it up, detesting the false cheeriness in my voice when I answered. After a while I stopped returning calls from my girlfriends. I didn't want to talk to anyone, so it was easier to let the phone keep ringing.

Peter was unaware of my performance because I was an expert at hiding behind masks. I couldn't admit to him that I was a failure, and that I was letting him, our baby and our brand-new family down. I was frightened when work took him away from home for more than a night, and he travelled interstate and overseas a lot. Peter was happy with our beautiful new family, attentive, caring and besotted with our new daughter. How could I tell him what I was feeling? I was ashamed and drowning in guilt. How could I confess that I was falling apart when finally I had my fairy-tale ending? Peter didn't sense that anything was awry with his wife as I appeared to be in control and sticking to the routine that Chris, the mothercraft nurse, had been helping me organise.

I kept writing down 'useful' information in a large diary. There was so much to remember, so much to write down, because I had to make sure I was doing everything the 'right' way. I had to get it all on paper before I could get any sleep. What side had I finished feeding Allegra on? Was my breast drained of milk? And if it wasn't properly drained, would I get mastitis again? Did Allegra have a wet or dry nappy? How long had she slept for? Was it time to wake her up yet? How did I know how long to feed her? One of the midwives at the baby health clinic told me I should feed for at least fifteen minutes on each breast.

I would gaze at the silver Tiffany clock on the side table watching the second hand, tick, tick, tick. Time would slow down, dragging its silver hand through pain, blood and tears.

Why didn't Allegra open her mouth wide enough? How could I get her to attach properly? What was wrong with me? Why couldn't I do it?

'It's okay to top Allegra up with formula. My wife fed all of our babies on formula. She had problems breastfeeding. And our babies are all fine,' the paediatrician, Dr Barry Duffy, said. He had been looking after Allegra since she was born but I had booked some extra appointments with him as I worried about my daughter's low body weight. Dr Duffy was pointing out to me where Allegra's weight fitted on a chart compared to other babies of a similar age. She was below the curve and I could feel that panic rising again. He gently suggested giving Allegra more formula to get her weight closer to what it should be. All I could hear was what a failure I was, unable to feed my baby properly.

Dr Duffy interrupted my destructive daydreaming to ask how I was, and by the way he asked I knew he wasn't going to be fobbed off with a simple 'I'm fine' answer. He suggested in a non-intrusive way that I needed to look after myself and that I didn't have to put on a show for people around me. I knew as he looked into my eyes he could see the sparkle was just a trick of the light. I put my sunglasses on quickly to stop him looking past my carefully constructed facade.

I could feel the pane of glass thickening between myself and the rest of the living, breathing world. I was trapped behind it, distant, removed and numb. The world was living, breathing and laughing without me in it. My tears fogged up my sunglasses as I stumbled out of the children's hospital, still struggling with the baby capsule. Allegra was asleep, dancing in her dreams. I love you, my darling, I love you. I am trying. Please hang in there with me, baby girl, I whispered as we drove home to another long, lonely night.

Peter was travelling again for work and I had organised for my youngest sister, Claudia, to come and stay while he was away. I wondered if I could talk to her? Although she was my baby sister, Claudia always had the wisest words for all of our family. But I didn't speak up, scared that if I put a voice to my thoughts I would spiral out of control. Instead I tried to focus on the delicious chicken pie and creamy mashed potato she had cooked for me. Comfort food to soothe my soul.

No amount of comfort could get that pane of glass to shatter, however, but somehow I managed to keep smiling behind it. Each day I went through my list of tasks, dutifully noting everything down in my diary; it was my way of trying to stay in control while my mind spun faster and faster. Guilty, bad mother—I had my longed-for baby but I had never felt so wretched before. What right did I have to feel like this? I had plenty of support around me. A caring, extended family who often come around for visits, bringing supplies of good coffee and ready-made meals. We had the money to pay for extra help: Christina, our cleaner, mopped the floors and scrubbed the bathroom so the house was tidy. We were not battling to pay our mortgage or put food on the table. I had it easy, nothing to complain about. This mental soundtrack added an extra layer of guilt to the heaviness of my heart.

The mothercraft nurse, Chris, was still visiting each week. Another of her colleagues, Cheryl, also dropped over to sit with me while I breastfed. She softly suggested it might be time to stop and give myself a break. But I didn't want to stop trying to breastfeed as I was fixated on doing it 'properly'. We had a nursery full of cuddly pink teddy bears, drawers of folded flowery jumpsuits and presents wrapped in clear cellophane and tied in pink ribbon still waiting to be opened. But it was not enough to break the glass.

My coping mechanism for dealing with my mother's bipolar as a child meant I was good at pretending life was perfect. I had already fooled Peter, my sisters and girlfriends that I was revelling in being a mother. It was easy to fool the new clinic nurse during our regular appointments at the baby health clinic, too. She was even feeding me my lines.

'Oh, you're very different off the television, aren't you?' she said.

'Um, well, you know about the wonders of make-up and a good blow-dry. At work I have an amazing make-up artist to do my face each day. They put on false eyelashes too,' I said.

'What about the clothes that you wear on the television, do you get to keep them?'

'Most of them. Aren't I lucky? Not that I'm wearing them much at the moment!'

'Okay, let's take a look at this baby of yours. Take off her jumpsuit, and we'll put her on the scales.'

I stopped with my patter, willing the number on the scales to have increased since I weighed Allegra last night.

'She's still underweight. How are you going with the breastfeeding?'

'Alright, and the nipple shields are helping.'

'Good work.'

The nurse handed over a form for me to fill out, a checklist for postnatal depression. Known as the Edinburgh test, all new mums have to complete it either in the hospital or at the baby clinic. I returned to my script again, joking about the struggles of collapsing the pram to get it into the boot of the car. With a black felt-tipped pen I circled the 'correct' answer to every question.

I have been able to laugh and see the funny side of things

⓪ As much as I always could

1 Not quite so much now

2 Definitely not so much now

3 Not at all

I have blamed myself unnecessarily when things went wrong

3 Yes, most of the time

2 Yes, some of the time

① Not very often

0 No, never

I have been anxious or worried for no good reason

⓪ No, not at all

1 Hardly ever

2 Yes, sometimes

3 Yes, very often

I didn't miss a beat as I worked my way through the checklist.

I have felt scared or panicky for no very good reason

3 Yes, quite a lot

2 Yes, sometimes

1 No, not much

⓪ No, not at all

I have been so unhappy that I have had difficulty sleeping.

3 Yes, most of the time

2 Yes, sometimes

① Not very often

0 No, not at all

I was in a serious case of denial because the truth was far too scary, and it would have been a sign of failure and weakness, and that was not me. But it didn't matter how many 'correct' responses I circled, that thick pane of glass still would not shift and in fact became murkier and harder to see through.

Peter was away again, filming a story for *60 Minutes*, and I was robotically going through my daily routine. As he was flying through some time zone to meet up with a movie star at the Beverley Wilshire in Los Angeles, I sat in my usual spot on the couch, expressing milk using my brand-new breast pump. Allegra had just gone down for her morning sleep, and I wanted to make sure I was keeping up my breast milk supply. The phone rang, and for once I decided to answer it. On the other end of the line was the head of beyondblue, the support organisation for sufferers of depression, asking if I would be prepared to accept a role as a patron of its perinatal program. The timing of the call was extraordinary, as the organisation's head had no idea I was struggling with my sanity. No one did. Mum and I had done a lot of advocacy work for beyondblue so I had established a close relationship with it over the years. It was ironic, that much of this work included public speaking, carrying the message that there should be no shame or stigma attached to mental illness. And here I was burning with that very shame I had railed against. I confirmed that I would love to help out, and asked that some information be sent to me about the program.

Two days later a parcel arrived in the letterbox, and inside there was a checklist of symptoms for postnatal depression (PND).

If you have experienced some of the following symptoms for two weeks or more, it's time to get help:

- low mood and/or feeling numb
- feeling inadequate, like a failure, or feeling guilty, ashamed, worthless, hopeless, helpless, empty or sad
- often feeling close to tears
- feeling angry, irritable or resentful (e.g. feeling easily irritated by your other children or your partner)
- fear for the baby and/or fear of being alone with the baby or the baby being unsettled
- fear of being alone or going out
- loss of interest in things that you would normally enjoy
- insomnia (being unable to fall asleep or get back to sleep after night feeds) or sleeping excessively, having nightmares
- appetite changes (not eating or over-eating)
- feeling unmotivated and unable to cope with the daily routine
- withdrawing from social contact and/or not looking after yourself properly
- decreased energy and feeling exhausted
- having trouble thinking clearly or making decisions, lack of concentration and poor memory
- having thoughts about harming yourself or the baby, ending your life, or wanting to escape or get away from everything.

I answered yes to most of these questions—but I couldn't have PND, could I? That soundtrack kept whirring around in my head. What did I have to be miserable about? I had a supportive husband, a wonderful family . . . I was one of the lucky ones. I wasn't a single mum, or struggling financially. I was middle class with nothing to whinge about, and I had a wardrobe full of fabulous shoes. But none of that made the pane of glass go away. I told myself to get over it. I hid the beyondblue booklet away in my top bedside drawer, thinking that would silence the negative thoughts. Close it up, lock it away, shut up. Everything will be alright.

There is something about the dead of night that conjures up feelings of dread inside me. I hated sitting on the couch trying to breastfeed while outside it was pitch-black, not a star in the sky. Quiet, oh so quiet. The only sound I could hear was the ticking of the silver clock, the second hand not moving fast enough to get me out of the scary night-time world. I wrapped my baby girl up into her parcel of love and lay her back in her cot. Such a good girl, she slipped off to sleep quickly. But I went back to bed full of dread, knowing I would lie there for hours, unable to sleep. Exhausted, every pore of my being wanted to drift off into a gentle cottonwool sleep. Instead I was high on adrenaline, buzzy and wired, unable to turn off the thoughts whizzing around and around in my head. My brain would not switch off. I was scared. I had never felt so tired, but still I could not sleep. All I could do was think, think, think. Tick, tick, tick.

At last I could see flecks of mauve and pink light burning away the night sky. The kookaburras mocked me with their easy laughter. I had survived another night and during the daylight hours I could push the crazy thoughts away. The beyondblue booklet remained tucked away at the back of my top drawer, and I would ignore it for another day. Instead I distracted myself with a walk around the neighbourhood, pushing the immaculate pram with my beautiful baby. My props were my clothes, my smile and my sunglasses.

But when night came around again there was no protection, and I was unmasked by the darkness. There was nowhere for me to hide from my thoughts. The silver hand on the clock ticked relentlessly. I watched it creep around as I stroked the top of my darling daughter's head. I looked at that perfectly round clock and pondered how easily it could smash my daughter's skull, worrying at how it could slip from the table and the damage it could cause. I lay in bed and thought about that silver Tiffany clock while Allegra slept happily and innocently through the night.

Then I started thinking about the carving knife in the second drawer in the kitchen. It could so easily pierce my daughter's delicate skin. My mind kept returning to the wooden handle of the knife, the long blade. I was losing my mind, I was turning into my mother. I hated the nights, and it got to the point where I didn't want to go through another night with these thoughts. I could get through the day, but I couldn't get through the night. It wasn't long before those obsessive thoughts snuck into the daylight too. Tick, tick, tick.

I remember as a teenager when Mum and I would sit together under the flame tree in the hospital grounds, a small patch of green to escape the endless grey corridors of the psychiatric ward. I worried Mum would never leave this place, both this place of nothingness in her mind and the grimy room just next to the nurses' station at the top of the stairs. Mum told me that she too was frightened she would never get out of here. She didn't ever tell me she would kill herself, but when I left her in the cool shade of the tree one afternoon, one of her closest friends suggested to me that it might be easier for her if we could just let her go. I was shocked by the suggestion. I was never going to let her give up: she couldn't give up on us, she couldn't give up on herself.

The next day when I came to visit after school I found Mum lying on her bed, face turned to the wall. She wouldn't turn to look at me when I arrived, couldn't string a sentence together. The electroconvulsive treatment was playing havoc with her memory and she couldn't remember who I was. I sat on the edge of her unmade bed and gently stroked her hair. It seemed neither of us had words, but I wanted her to know that I was there and wasn't going anywhere.

And now that I was a mother I had truly lost my words. I didn't know how to speak up and get help and I feared that I might give up. Would the dread of the dark sweep me away? The more I tried to push the thoughts away, the harder it became. The daylight wasn't enough to save me. I knew there was something very wrong with me. Would I have to go to hospital? Would my baby be taken from me? Would the pane of glass pierce my body and make me bleed?

There were no stars out tonight. Usually I could look up at the summer night sky and feel anchored by the pinpricks of silver reaching out to me, but what had happened to the fistful of stars I could hang my wishes on? This evening there was no light, just a vast black sky that left me feeling icy cold. Unless I could find that silver lining again I would suffocate. I could no longer fight away the terrifying thoughts on my own. I wanted my mummy because I knew she would understand.

The next morning I called Mum on the phone, unable to reveal my fears to her face to face. But I knew I had to talk to her as I couldn't face another night like that. I counted the rings, half hoping it would go straight through to her voicemail. If it did

I could put on my chirpy voice and put off this conversation for a little longer. However, once I heard Mum's warm voice I realised there was no room for small talk. I had done enough of that and for too long. I needed to jump straight in before I lost my nerve.

'Mum, remember how you told me when I was a baby that you used to wonder what would happen if you let go of my head when you were giving me a bath?

'Oh yes, I remember. But why are you asking?' she said.

'Mummy, I'm so afraid. I can't do this anymore . . .'

'Do what?'

'I'm having bad thoughts,' I stammered.

'Like what?' she persisted, with concern now creeping into her voice.

'I keep thinking about the silver clock.' I knew I wasn't making sense, but I wasn't brave enough to tell her the whole story, or about the knife.

But somehow Mum knew what I was saying. 'Jessica, you do know that I didn't want to let you go in the bath, don't you? I would never let you go! I just worried about what would happen if I did and couldn't push the idea away. So I stopped giving you a bath and used a face washer to freshen you up. But the more I told myself not to think these hideous thoughts, the more they obsessed me.'

'My thoughts won't go away,' I whispered, while my throat filled with tears. 'I keep thinking about what the clock could do to Allegra. It might slip from the table while I'm breastfeeding and smash her head.' I couldn't hold it together any longer. I started to weep.

'They're only thoughts, Jessica. You know you would never do anything to harm yourself or Allegra. Why don't you give me the clock? It might be a way to stop giving it so much power. But you do need to tell Peter, and you must talk to your doctor too. Promise me you'll do that.'

'I promise. I love you, Mum.'

'Not as much as I love you, my darling.'

Mum came around straight after the phone call. She hugged me while I breathed in her familiar smell, then she stroked my head as I lay down in her lap. While my mother comforted me, my baby girl slept in her cot. I don't know how long we stayed on the couch. We didn't speak, we didn't need words. All I needed was the safety of Mum's understanding. Before she left I gave her the clock, which she slipped into her handbag. She made me promise again to talk to my doctor and to tell Peter as she would be checking up on me the next day.

That night, while the house slept, I wrapped the carving knife in old newspaper and threw it into the green wheelie bin. The garbage was being collected that morning, and soon the knife would be compacted in the back of the truck. But hiding the evidence didn't make me feel any better, instead I just felt ashamed. I was a crazy lady, a mad, bad mother. The obsessive thoughts kept running on a loop through my mind. I worried about what might happen to Allegra. I worried that the world was not a safe place for her, that I wouldn't be able to protect her. The pane of glass between me and everyone else was stuck fast.

'Pussycat, where's that silver clock?' asked Peter.

'What clock?'

'You know, the one we got as a present at Nicole's wedding. I haven't seen it on the bookshelf for a while.'

'No idea.'

'Can you look for it?'

I knew I had to confide in Peter about my despair, but I was afraid to tell him about the clock and the knife. It had been five days since Mum had taken the clock and she had been coming around each day to keep me company while Peter was at work. In the deepest part of myself, I knew they were just thoughts, only thoughts, and that I would never hurt Allegra or myself. But I didn't understand where these obsessive thoughts had come from and what they meant for me and my future. I was truly afraid that I now had a lifetime struggle with mental illness ahead of me. I had watched my whip smart mother reduced to a shadow of herself during episodes of her illness. I did not want that life. I had always thought my stubborn, strong-willed personality and permanent optimism would protect me. Instead my emotion-proof armour was now my undoing. I was on my knees, wondering if I would ever get up again.

'You are going so well. I am so proud of you,' Peter said cheerily after we had finished eating dinner in front of the latest episode of *Grey's Anatomy*. Each night we watched an episode from the boxed DVD set of the series, a routine that had started soon after we brought Allegra home from the hospital. I had cooked Peter's favourite meal of schnitzel and mashed potato. A rocky road chocolate bar was waiting in the fridge for dessert.

I knew this was my moment, my time to say something, tick, tick, tick. I had to finally put a voice to what was whirring around in my head.

'I'm not,' I blurted out. 'I'm not coping. I'm afraid that I have postnatal depression. I am so, so sorry.' Tears ran down my face.

Peter was silent for a moment, then he looked at me, his clear blue eyes filled with worry. 'You're not going to hurt yourself, are you?'

'No,' I replied.

'You're not going to hurt Allegra? Promise me you wouldn't hurt her!' he said urgently.

'No. *No!*' I *knew* I would never hurt my baby, but I was terrified of the thoughts in my head. I could not tell Peter about those yet. I doubted I could ever confess them to anyone.

Peter took me in his arms and held me tight while I buried my face in his shoulder. 'I know what we'll do.' My darling husband had already slipped into his fix-it mode. It was just what I needed to hear. 'I'll ring Jan, the obstetrician, tomorrow and you can go in and talk to her. It's okay. It's going to be okay,' he said.

For the first time in a long time I felt safe. I believed my husband's words of reassurance, and through that pane of glass I could feel his heart beating.

The next morning I went back to see our obstetrician, Dr Jan Dudley. Peter and I called her Cuddly Dudley, as she had a warmth, earthiness and kindness that made you want to hug her after each appointment. When I walked into her rooms, sat on that familiar chair, and looked at the small grey sculpture of a pregnant woman and the photos of her blonde daughters on her desk, I knew I could exhale, just a little.

Jan held my hand as I confessed my terrible thoughts. I told her I was afraid I was turning into my mother and I didn't want that to be my future, my family's future. I wanted to be the best mother I could be and did not want to let my baby girl or my husband down. She made an appointment for me to see a psychiatrist, a specialist in postnatal depression, the very next day. Ever so slightly I felt the crushing weight on my shoulders lift for a moment. I had finally given voice to my black thoughts, and as those thoughts bounced against the glass, they lost some of their fierceness.

I dressed deliberately for my meeting with Dr Marie-Paule Austin, choosing a brown cotton fifties-style dress with a diamond pattern, silver glitter ballet flats and pink lipstick. I kept looking down at my silver shoes as I sat in the white architectural-looking chair in Dr Austin's rooms. How I wanted to click my heels, Dorothy style, and vanish from this reality. There was a box of tissues on a side table nearby, and as I looked up at the doctor I smiled one of my practised smiles.

'Hello, thank you for seeing me,' I said.

'You can stop pretending,' replied Dr Austin.

'Pretending?'

'Tell me what's been happening.'

I told Dr Austin about my worries for Allegra, my problems breastfeeding, losing my job, Mum's illness and my obsessive thoughts.

'But that's normal,' Dr Austin said.

'Normal—what? Is it normal to have images of clocks and knives going around on a constant loop in your brain?'

'Yes, it is normal for someone who has postnatal depression,' Dr Austin continued. 'Obsessive, unpleasant thoughts are very common in people with PND.'

'I would never hurt Allegra.'

'I know that.'

'And I would never hurt myself.'

'I know that.'

'So why is it happening to me? Where have these thoughts come from?'

'Because your mind has been working in a panicked and anxious state, normal objects that you deal with every day can start to become sinister,' explained Dr Austin. 'You start misinterpreting things like the clock and the knife, things that you have used for a long time without having any problems. Because of the way your brain has been working, such objects start to appear hazardous and dangerous to your baby. The world becomes a very scary place because you want to do everything to protect your child—you are so intent on looking after her and keeping her safe that everywhere you look there is danger.'

'So I'm not a crazy lady.'

'No, but you do have an illness, postnatal depression.'

'I'm worried it's bipolar disorder—am I turning into my mother?'

'It's not bipolar, that is a totally different illness to PND,' Dr Austin reassured.

'I can't sleep.'

'That's because you have anxiety, and your body is operating on high levels of adrenaline and is ready to fight or flight.'

'So what can I do?' I asked pleadingly. 'I want to be better—I want to be me again.'

'There are a couple of treatment options, medication is one.'

'Will that get rid of the thoughts?' I persisted.

'Yes, there are particular medications that are good at helping with that and dealing with anxiety.'

'Okay, when can I start? Can I get a prescription? How long will it take to work?'

Dr Austin laughed. 'I don't think I've ever had a patient so eager to start medication. Normally I have to convince them.'

I didn't have a problem taking medication because I'd seen the difference psychiatric drugs had made to Mum's life, their complex biochemistry adjusting the chemical imbalance in her brain. Various combinations of drugs had really saved her life, even if it took a long time for doctors to find the right medication for her over the years.

On my way home from the appointment I stopped off at the pharmacy to get the antidepressants. I marked the date down in my diary with a star as I swallowed down my first tablet. Day one of starting again. Day one of cleaning that grubby pane of glass.

Me, aged 1. Already a cat lover.

Aged 3 and ready to help.

A budding ballerina! Aged 9, 1979.

Harriet (left), Claudia (right), Mum and me (middle)
in 1979 just before Mum's first breakdown.

Sisters. Claudia, Harriet and me in 1980 soon
after our parents separated.

A naughty teenager.

With Mum at my farewell dinner on the eve of going to uni, 1989.

My first day at uni in Bathurst.

I did it! With Mum on my graduation day, 1993.

Working at Prime TV, Canberra, 1993. With Melissa Doyle.

Visiting Phillip Island and homesick in 1994.

On the *Channel Ten News* set, 1997.

Paris, 2002. I was sure Peter would propose here, but he didn't.

Our engagement party, Clovelly, 2003.

Going crazy with my sisters on the morning of my wedding, 12 January 2004.

Mum and my mother-in-law Charlotte Overton at our wedding.

My dad and step-mum, John and Lesley Rowe, at our wedding.

Our cat wedding cake!
Audrey is on the top
and Alfie is climbing
up the side.

The happy couple, the day after our wedding.

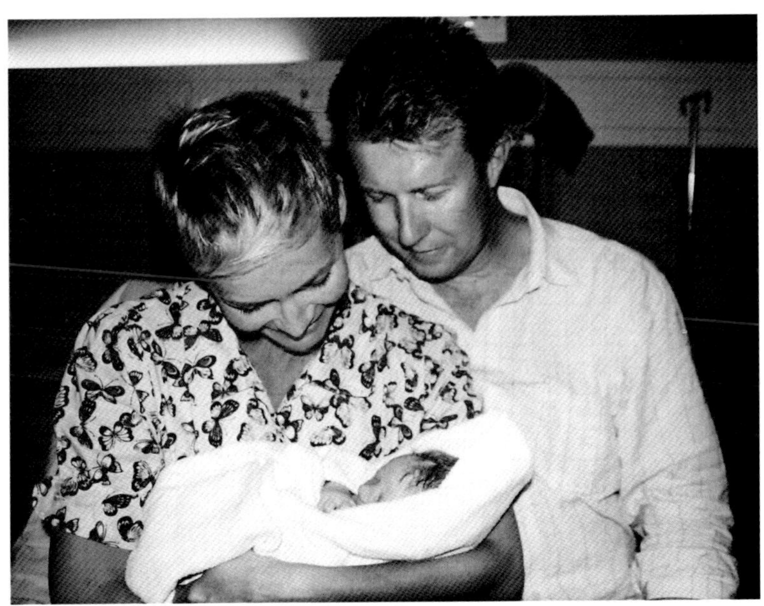

Allegra arrives, 18 January 2007.

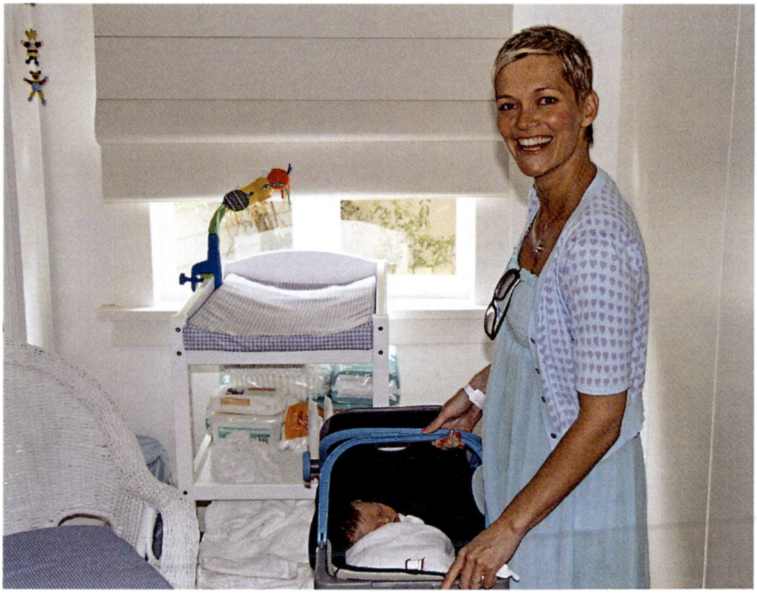

Allegra comes home.

Still struggling to breast feed.

Back at work, December 2007. Allegra watches on.

Allegra's first birthday.

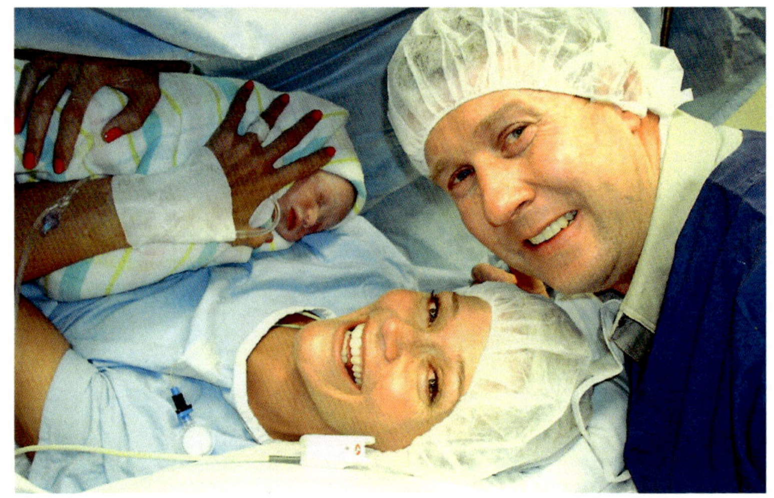

Welcome to the world Giselle, 9 April 2009.

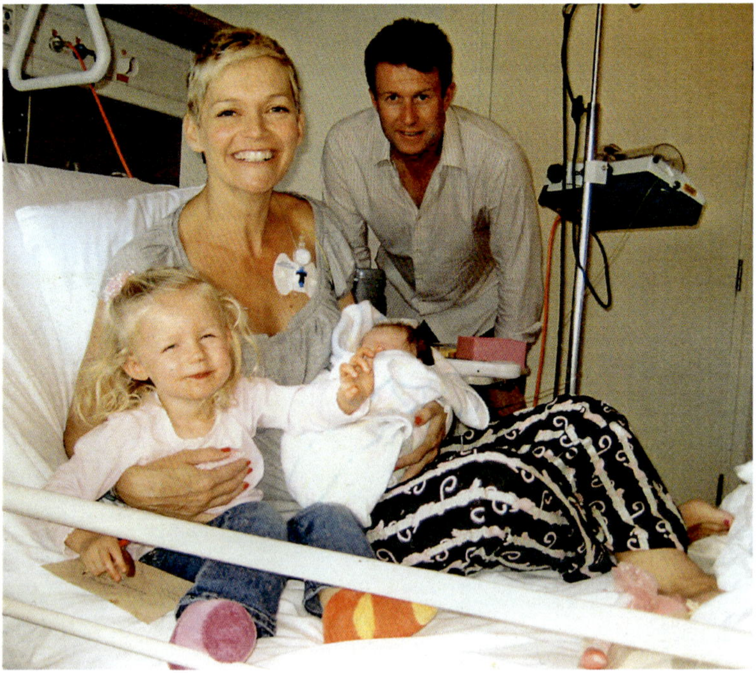

Allegra meets her baby sister Giselle.

With Mum, Harriet and all the kids.

Giselle and Allegra keeping my dad busy.

Giselle and Allegra give my gown the thumbs up.

Allegra and Giselle.

Special times with Peter.

Our gorgeous family.

With the *Studio 10* crew . . . Joe Hildebrand, Ita Buttrose and Sarah Harris.

Giselle and Allegra on suitcase watch and keeping their dad at home.

CHAPTER NINE

The turquoise salt water rushed up to my feet. I turned around, squinting into the sunlight, to wave at Harriet where she sat under the shade of the beach tent, Allegra next to her on a frangipani-patterned towel. It was my first ocean swim since my daughter was born and I waded tentatively into the deeper water. Big waves have always frightened me, but I am also drawn to the cleansing, calming effect of the sea. Diving under the first wave, I squeezed my eyes shut and waited for the surge to wash over me. I stood up with my eyes still closed, gently rubbing them until the sting of salt water forced them open. Fine soft sand flicked out from under my feet as I walked back up the beach to the stripy tent, the sun on my back transforming drops of seawater into splotches of glittery salt.

These exquisite, sharp sensations seem to thaw out my frozen body. I am gradually becoming myself again.

It's only two weeks since I started taking the antidepressants. Standing on the front lawn back at our house there is the scent of jasmine in the breeze, the sweet, heady smell of summer tickling my nose and making me sneeze. I love this fragrance; it makes me think of sand, sunshine, hot concrete, lemonade icy poles and cool blue water. I haven't smelt this in a long time, even though the vines have been flowering along our back fence since I brought Allegra home.

My baby girl has been doing everything right, sleeping, putting on weight and making my heart sing. There is no more breast-feeding; bottle-feeding is working a treat as Peter, my mum and in-laws can now give Allegra her milk. I'm able to untether a little from the crushing responsibility I've been feeling for this sweet soul and now I can exhale as I walk down the street on my own. And it feels good.

When I notice that sweet smell of jasmine, there's a flickering deep inside of me, like a butterfly beating its wings. What is it? It feels like hope. A change in the breeze, a chance to breathe out and exhale just a little more. And as I take a breath I feel like I am returning to my body. Closing my eyes, I drink in the new feeling of lightness, a little like I'm emerging from a cocoon into the bright, white light.

The dead of night frightens me less and less. My obsessive thoughts start to fade to grey, until they have totally disappeared. I kiss the top of Allegra's soft, sweet head, inhaling her very essence. The snuffling sounds she makes as she breathes in and out tell me she's hungry, and that no longer fills me with anxiety at the thought of trying to feed her. Now I delight at the way she rubs her eyes when she's tired, in exactly the same way that her father does. Her beautiful mouth opens wide, copying mine, as we laugh together when I hold her aloft under the bright blue sky. I forget what life was like before she was around. It's like she has always been here.

The weeks flew by and the scent of jasmine and gardenias had now faded from the garden as we stood again on the lawn, my high heels sinking into the soft winter grass. We were christening Allegra, beloved family and friends by our side, and Reverend Crews, who married us, on duty again. The reverend began by telling the story of an African tribe, and as he spoke he poured a small amount of blessed Sydney tap water onto our daughter's head. The story went something like this one, which is retold by Jack Kornfield in his book *A Path with Heart*.

'There is a tribe in east Africa in which the art of true intimacy is fostered even before birth. In this tribe, the birth date of a child is not counted from the day of its physical birth nor even the day of conception, as in other village cultures. For this tribe the birth date comes the first time the child is a thought in its mother's mind. Aware of her intention to conceive a child with a particular father, the mother then goes off to sit alone under a tree. There she sits and listens until she can hear the song of the child that she hopes to conceive. Once she has heard it, she returns to the village and teaches it to the father so that they can sing it together as they make love, inviting the child to join them. After the child is conceived, she sings it to the baby in her womb. Then she teaches it to the old women and midwives of the village, so that throughout the labour and at the miraculous moment of birth itself, the child is greeted with its song. After the birth all the villagers learn the song of their new member of their tribe and sing it to the child when it falls or hurts herself. It is sung in times of triumph, or in rituals and initiations. The song also becomes a part of the marriage ceremony when the child is grown, and at the end of life, his or her loved ones will gather around the deathbed and sing this song for the last time.'

The story's sentiments resonated deep inside me. My tears fell onto my daughter's flushed cheeks, as I looked down at her in my arms. Allegra looked away, her attention drawn to the fairy beams of sunlight reflecting off the embroidered lace of her christening gown, and her tiny fingers went back to fiddling with the ends of the long white ribbons that her godmother, Annebelle, had painstakingly stitched onto the puffy sleeves of the gown.

My tears continued to fall as I thought about the circle of love around us both, a circle that I had almost broken because I was too ashamed to admit that I wasn't coping. I had walked away from my village when I needed it most. On that crisp, ice blue afternoon it now stood next to me on the lawn and joined in our song of love, hope and second chances. And as the afternoon turned colder, I wrapped Allegra in a white mohair rug and she beamed as she was passed around her village.

Although I had told my family about the postnatal depression and the medication I continued to take, I still hadn't revealed the depths of my illness.

It had been hardest telling my father and stepmother as they didn't agree with my decision to take antidepressants. They were worried about the side-effects of such drugs. They did, however, give me plenty of hands-on support with their love, concern, endless babysitting and enthusiasm for Allegra. My sisters understood and kept up their unconditional love. My in-laws came around often to take Allegra and me out on walks around the neighbourhood. It was a relief to have their companionship and understanding. And the biggest relief was I no longer had to keep up my happy mother appearance. Finally being honest with those closest to me was liberating.

But I still couldn't reveal the whole truth, as a part of me was ashamed of where my mind had taken me in those dark months.

Mum knew more of the full story than anyone else, even Peter. The pane of glass was still there, but it locked me away from the rest of the world less and less. It didn't frighten me anymore as I now knew I had the power to wipe it clean and even make it disappear eventually. The chill I once felt in the dead of night had disappeared and had now been replaced by a peace and calmness that I revelled in.

In the hours before dawn, Allegra often enjoyed her bottle of formula while I watched reality television shows like *Extreme Makeover*, *Trinny and Susannah Undress the Nation* and *The Girls of the Playboy Mansion*. The glow of the television flickered off the walls as she fell asleep against my chest, and I wanted to tattoo this feeling of contentment into my heart. I was happy. Once the Playboy bunnies had got out of their Ugg boots and into their four-poster beds, I'd put Allegra down in her cot and creep back into bed next to Peter, falling into a deep, blissful sleep.

My head was in a better place but I still felt bitter and resentful about what had happened to my career over the past year. Now that my mental health had stabilised I was in a stronger place to consider what I might do with the professional side of my life. I worried that my prospects for working in the media again had been destroyed and feared that I wasn't any good at my job anyway. It was hard to ignore the voice whispering nastily in my head that I was a has-been. Maybe the television critics were correct; for the first time in my life I started to seriously question my career-minded self.

Since becoming a mother I had changed forever. Some of those changes I embraced, but the shifts in my career goals

I was still struggling to reconcile. There was no doubt that I had lost my confidence, and this desperation to still have value in the professional world led to me agreeing to be part of a reality television show, *Dancing with the Stars*. Ignoring the advice of my husband, who said I should lie low, I convinced myself that this job would be my only chance at a media comeback. It also fitted in with my lifetime philosophy that it was always worth giving something a go and taking a risk.

'Ladies and gentlemen, please welcome to the floor Jessica Rowe and her partner, Serghei Bolgarschii.'

Serghei grabbed my hand as we walked in darkness to our places on the dance floor. Wearing a catsuit and black sequinned pussycat ears, I sat on the bottom of the stairs and carefully arranged my feather boa tail behind me to avoid any tripping hazards once we started our dance routine. The piano began to play and I stretched my black-gloved hand out to Serghei.

Thankfully my brain was on autopilot, the twenty hours of foxtrot rehearsals that week meaning I didn't forget the routine. I stopped counting each step and started to really enjoy the sensation of sliding, stretching and spinning across the dance floor. The song was 'Love Cats' by The Cure, one of my favourite dance tracks as a pimply teenager. I let the words wash over me as I brought my 'paw' up to rub my sparkling ears. I could do this! I gave my sexiest look down the camera lens before trailing off in the other direction, my feathery tail slinking behind me.

The judges liked our performance and we scored the highest points of the evening. For me, taking this role on *Dancing with the Stars* was a way of blasting the pane of glass away forever, although scaring myself witless on national television with the accompanying risk of public humiliation may have been an extreme way of doing it. I also wanted to show all those people who didn't believe in me that I hadn't disappeared. If I won the contest, I figured it would reinvigorate my career and sense of self-worth.

I trained with Serghei from 8.45am until 1pm every day in a mirror-panelled dance studio. Determined to be a good student, I focused on learning all my steps perfectly as well as trying to relax at the same time. But despite working hard, I was not what you would call a fast learner, and the blur of quicksteps, jives and lifts did not come easily to my sleep-deprived brain. My Russian dance partner's tough-love teaching style didn't help either, and he occasionally lost patience with me. How many times did he have to say heel first, not toe first! I had to keep reminding him that I wasn't a professional dancer but a journalist and a new mum who liked a sparkling costume. And thank goodness for the costumes—in the end it was the promise of wearing a dazzling gown, gloves and jewels that kept me motivated each week.

Cooking Allegra dinner at night, I marked out the dance steps on our narrow kitchen floor. Thankfully Peter was away a lot so I could be single-minded about trying to reinforce what I had learnt each day. The rehearsals were fun as it gave my days a structure far removed from sleep routines and mashed avocado. I enjoyed having a fresh purpose to focus on. Each evening I counted dance steps in my head before going to sleep, although there was always a point in the routine where I had a mental block and forgot what came next. I also got extreme stage fright whenever we had to perform in front of anyone else, a slight problem when I had to dance in front of a studio audience and television cameras each week! No wonder my dance teacher's blood pressure was rising.

Despite sometimes floundering on the dance floor, I did find my groove again, a confidence that had been missing for nine months. To my surprise I also found I could manage being apart from Allegra for a couple of hours each day. It was a treat to be doing something that was just for me. And with the help of my dad and stepmother, and later our wonderful nanny Libby, I was able to travel to Melbourne with Allegra for two nights each week for TV rehearsals and the live show. The pane of glass had finally gone and I was able to get on a plane with my baby, look out the window at the bright white clouds, stay in a hotel with her and leave her with babysitters while I embarrassed myself on national television.

Each Sunday evening before the live taping, I waited with Serghei next to the dusty black velvet curtain and felt sick. Rather than getting better each week, my mind seemed to empty of the steps I had to perform despite the hours of rehearsals. I had peaked too soon with my 'Love Cats' performance! What on earth was I doing here? I tried to calm myself by drawing on the advice of showbiz queen Patti Newton, my dressing room buddy, who told me 'you just have to let go'. I was ready to go alright—go right away from this curtain and bolt home, where I could be watching *The Real Housewives of Atlanta* while eating a block of Toblerone chocolate.

One of the bonuses of doing the show was meeting Olympic swimmer Elka Graham. We clicked straight away, and I loved her enthusiasm, naturalness and preoccupation with statistics. For Elka, every topic of discussion had a probability rating, a percentage of winning or losing. Her passion for numbers and precise details also helped with my stage fright. She had a wonderful knack of trying to distract me when she saw the panic start to flicker in my eyes, calming me down beautifully by asking me plenty of questions about Allegra.

Not surprisingly, it didn't last: I was voted out by week six or seven of the series. That night, after doing the samba and bungling all my steps, I kept up a smile for the cameras. Calling from home afterwards, Peter told me that he and our cats, Audrey and Alfie, had their paws over their faces, unable to watch as I stumbled my way through the routine. I tried to laugh at his description and my grin remained fixed at the after party as I guzzled down glass after glass of cheap champagne. Once I got back to my hotel room and peeled off my false eyelashes and long blonde wig, I howled with disappointment and relief in the bathroom. Standing in the hot shower, the water ran over my orange spray-tanned skin as my hot tears fell down the drain. I had desperately wanted to win, somehow believing that a trophy topped with a glitter mirror ball would save my career.

It was such a contradiction. No, *I* was the contradiction—determined to be taken seriously but still caught up in the empty appearances of success. Here I was, now a mother with a small baby but also with a long media career behind her, convinced that winning a dancing competition would resurrect my job prospects. Was I really that shallow? Sometimes. I had enjoyed the trappings of success, the gowns, the make-up and the attention. Who would I be without that life? Most of my 37 years had been taken up with 'making it', and now I didn't know if I would ever be there again. And who would I be, who was I, if I wasn't that person anymore?

However, as I wallowed in self-pity, my mother's no nonsense advice that she had repeated over the years kept going around and around in my head: 'But darling, no one ever said life was meant to be fair.'

'Can't it be fair just this once?' I wanted to scream.

A sore head and dried-biscuit mouth woke me up way too early the next morning. As I rolled over in bed, I spotted the smudges of dark make-up that I had left on my white hotel pillowcase. Allegra sensed my stirring and started whacking her cat cuddly against the side of the travel cot to get my attention. I smiled as her sparkling young eyes locked on to my tired old ones. I knew she wouldn't let me lie down in bed for much longer—she was ready for squishy-squashy vegemite toast for breakfast, washed down with pureed apple and yoghurt. Ugh.

Allegra was now nine months old and it didn't matter to her that her hungover mummy hadn't won a glitzy trophy. All my baby girl wanted was to start the day and discover what was waiting for her on the other side of the hotel room door. She was ready to sit in her stroller and explore the Botanical Gardens, our morning routine while we stayed in Melbourne. The cold morning air cut through my layers of clothing but the temperature didn't seem to bother Allegra. Every time I struggled to get her rainbow-striped knitted beanie firmly over her ears, she would quickly flick it off again.

'Allegra! Come on, cheeky chops, it's cold—keep your hat on for Mummy.' But again she would just pull it off with a laugh and throw it onto the path. The sound of my daughter laughing was the most wondrous sound in the world.

'Quack, honk, quack, honk,' I said, trying to mimic the musical call of the black swans. 'Oh look, sweet pea, see that baby one there? It's still grey and fuzzy, but it's going to grow up into a beautiful swan. Quack, quack, quack! I wish I had brought some of our old vegemite toast to feed those brown ducks over there—they look like they would love to try some.'

Past the duck pond, I pushed the stroller slowly up the path until we were beneath the giant Chilean wine palm. It was my favourite tree in the gardens and I rested my hand against its rough, solid trunk while holding the stroller with my other hand. Gazing up, bits of sunlight were trying to sneak through the enormous green fronds of the palm leaves.

'Look, my darling, see how high it stretches up into the big sky? Look how green its leaves are! Do you think we might see a cheeky monkey swinging up there?' I asked as Allegra once again threw her beanie onto the ground.

We moved quickly through the succulent garden, Allegra reaching out to squeeze the downy, innocent-looking cacti.

'Ooooh, ouch, they're sharp! Just look at their spikes, don't touch them, my darling.' But my warnings were ignored as Allegra tried to squirm out of the harness clipping her in.

As we made our way along the shady path I could see Allegra's little legs kicking out from the sides of the stroller. Her eagerness to be part of everything around her snapped me out of my self-absorption. I wanted to see the gardens through her eyes, new, fresh, exciting and unspoilt.

'Beautiful girl, look at those dark pink waterlilies on the pond. See how pale their petals are in the centre? Do you think Jeremy Fisher might be hiding under one of those lily pads? Perhaps he's still sleeping in with his other froggy friends at the edge of the pond. Do you know, I remember my mummy, your Marmi, taking me for walks around ponds just like these . . .'

My running commentary continued as we did our familiar loop through the gardens. I had become talented at this sort of one-way conversation. I remember reading in one of my baby books about how important it is to talk with your baby and it was easy for me to follow that particular piece of advice, because I did enjoy a chat.

But it was getting harder to keep up my running commentary while pushing Allegra up the hill as I was in desperate need of another coffee, or something sweet to eat. The cheap champagne had left my head throbbing, and the fresh Melbourne air was not blasting the fuzz out of my brain. The cool breeze was now just making my ears ache and head hurt even more. There was enough time for a final loop around the bottom of the War Memorial before getting a taxi to take us to the airport and back to our normal life.

Although I was busting to get home, I was unsure how I would deal with the shift back to my daily routine. The show hadn't ended the way I had hoped, but I loved the spunk and edge it had awakened inside of me. That night at home as I packed away the feathered black catsuit, carefully laying the black gloves and sequinned ears on top, I was afraid the renewed grind of domesticity might kill my new-found sparkle. I had been so relieved to discover that my naughty, cheeky side was still there and I didn't want to lose that glittery part of myself again.

CHAPTER TEN

Hot lusty sex sometimes needs time to percolate. It wasn't so easy to switch from domestic non-goddess to sex kitten in real life; getting in the mood to slip off your angel wings takes time and patience. For me, sex had lost its excitement and spontaneity, my desire over the past year dampened by sore and leaking nipples, exhaustion and large comfy Cottontails. The downside of juggling so much in my mind—like pureed meals, doctors' appointments and career limbo—meant there was little room left to contemplate the G spot. Surely it's still there, just a bit to the left? No, to the right. Don't stop, not yet, don't stop.

Sleep had become my new nirvana and bed was now my place to greedily grab some snatches of downtime. How much sleep I was or wasn't getting had become an obsession. I would quiz every woman I spotted with a pram and ask her the sleep question. Pretty much no one with a small baby was getting enough sleep—or if a new mum told me that her baby slept all night and she was getting lots of sleep, I now suspect she was lying.

Unfortunately for Peter, actually getting hot and heavy under the covers became a distant memory for a while. My sex drive cooled off even further because of the antidepressants I was still taking, so while the pane of glass had gone my libido had also been put on ice. And I was desperate to have my body to myself, even for a few hours, after being available to another little person 24 hours a day. I would hold my breath if Peter rolled over, stretching his arm over my waist.

'Can't you just hold me?' I asked.

'Oh but I know I can get you in the mood,' said Peter.

'Nothing will get me in the mood. Just give me a cuddle, I'm too tired . . . I love you.'

'But what about me?'

'Go and take a cold shower . . .'

My long-suffering husband would sigh, roll back over and turn on the radio. As he struggled to tune it in to a talkback station, the baby monitor playing havoc with the reception, I was already asleep and snoring. My heavy sleep would be undisturbed until I heard the sounds of my daughter snuffling through the monitor, ready for her early morning bottle.

Life slid back into a routine of sorts, after I had finished *Dancing with the Stars*, a routine that still didn't include having much energy for sex. I told myself that sex wasn't about how many times you 'do it' a week; that knee-buckling feeling between your legs can ebb and flow, but it needs time and the right head-space to be nurtured. I longed to rediscover the part of myself that melted at the right touch from my lover, but first I just needed to get some sleep.

I wondered, was anyone having sex? How were other mums coping with the changes in their bodies and the extra demands on their emotional energy? Was that mother with her toddler in the stroller who I saw each morning at the cafe too exhausted for sex too? Of course, the twenty-somethings draped over each other at the cafe bench would be having wild sex, probably after staying out late clubbing. In a galaxy far, far away, I was once a careless and carefree twenty-something too. But now?

Bad mother! What a wicked woman I was to be daydreaming like this. I was supposed to be grown up, responsible and sensible, but everyone I knew with babies and small children wasn't getting enough sleep or sex. It was hard to get in the mood for loving when little people were at you all day. Allegra's sweet face would be pressed up against the shower screen while I tried to take a second to meditate on the day ahead. She pulled on my legs, hid under my skirt and constantly demanded my attention. By the time the sun went down, all I craved in bed was white chocolate Lindt balls and a good Swedish thriller.

Work continued to take Peter overseas a lot, so Allegra and I spent our days walking the neighbourhood and visiting the local parks. Playgrounds became my least favourite place in the world—I would rather chew my own arm off than go to another park. The rest of the world seemed to be getting on with something really fascinating and I was stuck behind a wretched swing again. I missed the buzz of working in a television studio. There was nothing like the adrenaline of talking live on air, knowing there was only one chance to get it right. Even if you make a mistake you just had to keep on going. I missed talking to my colleagues, both on television and while we got ready behind the scenes. I missed the gossip, the laughs, the serious conversations about politics and the not so serious talk about whether leopard print is a classic and perfectly appropriate for news presenters to wear. (I'm still adamant that it is!)

But here I was in yet another windswept park, and I had never felt so bored or lonely. All the other mothers looked like they were having such a happy time in the sandpit. I smiled and waved, recognising some familiar faces from the park, looking desperately for an ally. Was I the only one feeling brain dead and dreaming of being somewhere else? Did I need to increase my medication or was it normal to feel like this? What use were the qualifications I had spent my adult life building up? Now I had a double degree in unloading the dishwasher and swing pushing. While the glass pane of depression had vanished, there was still resentment and restlessness fluttering inside me. I mourned the loss of my old self, the confident and self-assured woman I once was. Being a mother had broken my stride and I needed to work out how to get my groove back. I had wanted so desperately to be a mum, but nothing had prepared me for the hard slog and repetitiveness of real life. And here I was again, turning into one of those whingeing, ungrateful mothers I had promised myself I would never be.

I hadn't expected staying at home with my daughter to be a struggle. Sure there were moments of joy but it seemed like I had lived a lifetime each day. I changed endless nappies, wiped down benches, did incessant loads of washing, and built up stacks of blocks only to have them knocked down moments later. What would happen if I hid in the bathroom for a while to read a chapter of my book? Did I always have to be inventing new games? Did we have to play peekaboo again? I put extra pressure on myself to be in the moment as much as possible, probably because I was unconsciously trying to make up for the times that Mum hadn't been in the moment with me and my two sisters.

Life hadn't always been like this, of course. I had once been a sexy free spirit, a life that was light years away from me now. Squinting into the blazing sun at the playground, stars start to dance in front of my eyes and suddenly I am dancing on the top of a white marble bar on the Greek island of Santorini. After my fifth shot of something seductively sweet and strong, my inhibitions had been shed—in fact, they were shed several days ago when I first arrived in this indigo-blue paradise. No one knew me so I could be whoever I wanted, desirable, confident and indestructible. I'd been dancing all night then living on honey-drenched yoghurt for breakfast, snacking on creamy feta cheese, olives, thinly sliced onion and tomatoes for lunch, and downing any number of colourful cocktails for my dinner.

Each morning I woke up in my small cliff-top room, bright-eyed and clear-headed despite my nocturnal naughtiness. Wearing just bikini bottoms, I would roast my body under the cloud-free sky, oblivious to the strength of the Mediterranean sun. Lying on my blue-striped beach chair, rented for a handful of drachma a day, my bare skin was protected from the white pebbles of the beach and also gave my friend and me a lazy position from which to check out the handsome blokes on the beach. That summer we were young, untouchable and bulletproof.

My Greek island holiday came in the middle of a year of modelling in Europe. I use the word 'modelling' loosely, as that part of my career was limited to sporting and camping catalogues in Germany. An agency based in Munich had signed me up from Australia because it thought I had potential in the lucrative world of mail order catalogues and television commercials.

The highlight of my less than brilliant modelling career was starring in an ad for washing powder, in which I wore white underpants and a singlet while filling up the front-loading machine. It was so unremarkable that my part got cut from the ad before it even made it to television.

During the day I changed in and out of Gore-Tex mountaineering gear and tried to look convincing holding an ice-pick in the snow; the catalogue photographer said he wished I looked as relaxed on the top of the Alps as I did on the dance floor. I joked back that I had plenty of experience in clubs but knew next to nothing about climbing mountains. It was easier to pretend to be a camper, or a golfer, or a cyclist—anything high altitude was out of my comfort zone. There were no fancy fashion labels—the most stylish I got was wearing lilac checked golfing shorts with a matching mauve bucket hat—but I was earning good deutschmarks, far more money than the student living allowance that was deposited fortnightly into my bank account at home. The money I was earning would be enough to fund the rest of my studies, so although initially I had only planned to take a few weeks off, in the end I stayed on in Europe and deferred the final year of my communications degree.

Most of that time I was dancing in night clubs with my new-found friends, who had also temporarily left their homes and regular lives far behind. Once the sun went down, evenings were a blur of tequila shots, music and nightclubs. It was easy to make friends in this hothouse of hormones and youthfulness. I shared an apartment in Munich with Pierre, a French Canadian model who had dimples to die for and became my unrequited love; I decided he must be gay since I couldn't tempt him. We walked around holding hands or arm in arm and shared beds, but we each stayed chastely on our own side. We were best friends.

He would wipe away my tears when I missed out on another catalogue job or dinner date.

There was also Jane, a six-foot blonde amazon from New Zealand with a plummy accent, who I managed to lead astray most nights. She was the most sensible of our group, reining us in and telling us to get our beauty sleep if we were going to have a chance of getting a job. Jane knew how to rock a catwalk and spent many hours trying to teach me how to strut, swinging my hips and pointing my toes. Unfortunately her expertise and experience weren't enough to change my frog style of walking and put-on pout, which looked more like a comedy routine. Eventually Jane gave up her lessons and told me to stick to modelling sportswear and camping equipment.

My partner in crime and humour was Greg, a hair and make-up artist from Melbourne. The pair of us would often get stuck into the cheap apple schnapps for sale in the neighbourhood Spar supermarket, downing the small bottles of sickly sweet alcohol before reaching the checkout. He would buy my groceries or treat me to meals at glitzy restaurants when my finances couldn't stretch beyond breakfast cereal, trail mix and dark brown pumpernickel bread. Our shrieks of laughter and silly voices frequently attracted raised eyebrows and mutterings from the camel-coated, sensibly shod elderly German couples trying to walk past us on the icy footpaths.

Greg was the experienced one of the group, having already worked in Paris, London, Tokyo and New York. He was in Munich to make some fast money before heading back to get 'tear sheets' from the editorial work he was bound to be booked for in the Conde Nast fashion magazines. The closest I got to working for those magazines was when Greg would do my make-up for our nights out. He would darken my eyebrows and give me a wicked, wing-tipped black liquid eye line before I dressed in my new gold Lurex mini dress with black opaque tights and suede knee-high boots.

Our party pack was rounded out by Toni, another Aussie, who had long, languid limbs and a wicked laugh. She introduced me to the sounds of Depeche Mode, whose *Violator* album became the only cassette I would play in my Walkman. And she also showed me the pleasure of taking over the dance floor, something I would never have had the nerve to do in Sydney.

The nightclub of choice for our motley crew became P1, named after its address which was number one on the famous Prinzregentenstrasse. Absorbed in my wild new world, I was oblivious to the dark past of the location of our regular revelry. The club was housed in the museum known as the Haus der Kunst (literally the House of Art). Construction had begun on the neoclassical style building in 1933 using plans by Hitler's architect of choice, Paul Ludwig Troost. The colonnaded concrete edifice became the Third Reich's first monumental structure. If you looked closely at some ceiling panels at the front of the building you could still see lurid green and red swastika motif mosaics. Just a few years later, at the end of the Second World War, American forces used the building as their officers' mess, and it was during that time the address was shortened to P1.

In the early eighties, part of the museum was transformed into the P1 club, which became the most chic club in Germany. Mick Jagger, Milli Vanilli and Boris Becker all spent some time on its dance floor. Rumour was that Princess Stephanie of Monaco had once been turned away from the red velvet rope. But the most famous person I saw was a German beauty queen who, I was told, starred on the German version of the *Wheel of Fortune*.

Drinks were absurdly expensive, so we'd stock up on schnapps and gluhwein before heading out around eleven o'clock at night. We would get the train to Odeonsplatz station before walking the couple of blocks to the club. My snow leopard-print coat went some way towards keeping out the subzero temperatures during our perilous walk along the slippery footpaths, a toy koala backpack slung over my shoulder. I was a long way from home but I had never been happier in my young life.

Most Friday and Saturday nights the bar staff gave us free drinks, Midori and lemonade and other lolly-flavoured rocket fuel like flaming Sambuca and cheekily named cocktails. Our teeth glowed white as we tossed our heads back and danced under the fluorescent lights on the dance floor, the acid house music of The KLF throbbing through our bodies as we marvelled at our sophistication and style.

Around four in the morning the club closed and we returned to our tiny three-room flat at the top of an eight-storey apartment block. There was no lift, so it took time to make our way up the seemingly endless flights of stairs. We loudly announced our homecoming with the sound of our boots clomping on the stairs and our drunken laughter bouncing off the plaster walls, counting how many stairs we had left until we reached our attic apartment.

At that time my crush was Gary, a very tall, buff, curly-haired Californian model. Unfortunately he couldn't dance, but he was happy to watch me and my friends pretend to be the supermodels from George Michael's 'Freedom' video. Gary bought me drinks, made me laugh and was such a sweet, sweet man. We would hang out together during the day in Munich's central English Garden, sitting at long wooden benches under the Chinese Tower sipping steins of German beer. My favourite was the rich honey-coloured Weiss beer.

Gary and I shared stories about our families, our homes and our hopes for the future. Like many other male models, Gary really wanted to be an actor and was saving his modelling money for acting school and to keep himself solvent between jobs. I still dreamt of being a journalist but I wasn't in a hurry to return to my mundane life in Australia; I was far too absorbed with re-inventing myself and working out who and what I wanted to be.

Even though I wanted to keep travelling, I was forced to come home to Australia after twelve months away if I wanted to finish my degree. The university wasn't going to keep my place any longer.

And the girl who returned home to finish her studies was very different to the weary-looking 38-year-old who now sat in a children's playground wondering if all that excitement and wanderlust was long gone from her life. In her place was someone who was struggling to discover who she was now that she was a mother. Was that the sum of me? Did being a mum mean that I put my own needs behind everyone else's? Would it always be like this? Should I be happy with that? All of my attention and focus was being channelled into my daughter. I had become one of those helicopter parents I had read about, my senses on high alert to hover in and remove any obstacles in Allegra's way.

Peter and I made an effort to go out on dates again. Although I knew we needed to make special time together, most of our conversation over dinner centred around our daughter's milestones and his work.

'Allegra pulled herself up against the coffee table today—it won't be long before she starts taking steps on her own,' I said, juices from the san choy bow I was demolishing dripping down my hands.

'Really? Oh, I've been talking to Nick about the trip he wants me to do to Green Island. Apparently there is an incredible turtle migration that happens. The vision of baby turtles hatching and scrambling down the sand into the tropical water should be pretty incredible.'

'Uh-huh. Allegra also had fun playing with that farmyard set we got for her birthday.'

'I think we'll be leaving to do the story next week.'

'Oh—how long will you be going for?'

My world seemed to shrink as Peter's was ever-expanding, his work taking him to some of the most beautiful places on earth. And as my world got smaller, my ability to contribute meaningfully to any conversation outside of the world of babies was diminished. The few times we went out at night with other couples I found myself telling people about my husband's work exploits. What had happened to my adventures, my own anecdotes about life? If our cocktail party companions weren't parents it didn't take long for their eyes to glaze over when I explained I had a toddler; already they were looking over my shoulder to find someone more interesting to talk to. When Peter and I drove home from such a gathering I would sit silently in the car, fearful that I was turning into one of those tedious types who go on and on about their children.

In those quiet moments I also worried about my career. I was doing the occasional news-reading shift at Channel Seven when someone went on holidays. It was a part of my *Dancing with the Stars* deal, which I had hoped would unfold into a more permanent role with the Seven Network. It was a treat to spend time in the world of grown-ups as well as an opportunity to have my hair and make-up done and get out of my food-stained harem pants.

Slipping on new patent leather heels for work gave my confidence a boost. Having a bit of time away from children's playgrounds also gave me the energy to catch up with my girlfriend Georgia for nights out. Having first met at prenatal classes, the pair of us had been elbow-deep in purees and baby rusks for too long. One Thursday night I put on my black bodysuit with tight black Sass & Bide jeans and we tossed back glasses of pink champagne, laughing and sharing tales of our changed lives. When I got home later that evening I peeled off my shimmery jeans and felt sexy for the first time in ages. Peter lit up at the sight of my tipsy abandon. The pair of us laughed and kissed before we made love against the kitchen bench top.

Gradually a sense of equilibrium returned to me. I felt good marking down work shifts in my diary, having date nights with Peter and organising weekly pizza dinners with Georgia and our babies. Every Thursday afternoon Georgia and I would meet at the same park and compare notes about our week. Stretching out a picnic blanket, the pair of us would open the pizza box, greasy bags of hot chips and containers of deep-fried schnitzel. I could handle this park with Georgia; she was my mothers' group of one.

Georgia laughed with me when we spotted Allegra and her son, Nico, on top of the wooden pirate ship, the pair of them spinning the ship's plastic steering wheel wildly next to another little girl. It was no longer just me walking up to negotiate; Georgia was by my side as we managed to convince the kids to share the captain's duties. She was my partner in crime, and her likemindedness helped me to shrug off the glare of other mothers. At last I had found a friend who was like me.

CHAPTER ELEVEN

'When will you be home?'

'I'm in the Harbour Tunnel. If the traffic is okay, I should be there in about fifteen minutes,' Peter said, driving home from work on a Friday afternoon.

'Can you cancel our appointment?'

'No, we can't cancel Ross at the last minute. You're always cancelling things! Where are you? It sounds very echo-ey.'

'I'm in the toilet. I need to tell you something, and I'm not going to sit through an appointment with our accountant while I wait to talk to you.'

'Well, you're talking—talk to me now,' Peter replied calmly.

'Please cancel Ross,' I begged. 'We can do our tax return another time.'

'No, I'm not cancelling. Anyway, he just rang and he's parking outside our house now. What is it?'

'I don't want to do this over the phone,' I insisted.

'Just tell me!' Peter shot back, clearly getting frustrated by my evasiveness.

'Oh, alright then—I'm *pregnant*!' I shouted.

There was silence on the other end of the phone.

'What? How can that be possible?' Peter finally gasped.

'Well, we had sex.'

'I know that, Sherlock, but I thought we had to go through IVF again.'

'So did I, but it has happened naturally. It really is a miracle.'

I was still staring at the test stick when I hung up the phone on a now elated Peter. It was the third test I had done, with the third lot of fresh wee, and the results were the same: two blue lines. I was pregnant, *pregnant*! The test kit had been thrown in the supermarket trolley that morning along with the Weetbix, Lite milk, Caramello koalas and nappies. Allegra was swinging her little legs through the gaps of the trolley child seat and trying to grab a chocolate Kit Kat bar at the check-out as I tried to bury the pregnancy kit under the other items. The pregnancy test was my secret; I didn't really believe there was a new life growing inside of me. Anyway, I had drunk a little too much champagne the weekend before, and I wouldn't do that if I was pregnant.

My period was a couple of weeks late, but I told myself that didn't mean anything as I was used to having dodgy periods. Besides, it had been such a struggle to have Allegra that I didn't believe my body was capable of naturally conceiving a baby. A late period for me just meant a delay, an inconvenience before I could get started on IVF treatment again. Peter and I were ready to start trying for a second child to complete our family. We both had close relationships with our siblings and knew the joy they brought to our lives, so we wanted Allegra to experience that too if she possibly could. If my period didn't arrive naturally I could take some medication to bring one on, but Dr Tierney, the fertility specialist, wanted to wait until I got my period before we did the ultrasounds and blood tests to check everything was ready for a new round of treatment.

The appointment with our fast-talking accountant was a blur as he ran through balance sheets and interest rates. All I could hear were the two rainbow lorikeets squawking outside our front windows, their yellow-tipped beaks carefully gathering nectar from the red flowering eucalyptus tree. Their squawks became louder as a brave myna bird dared to get too close to their feast. As the technicolour pair flapped their vibrant green wings at the little bird, I felt the pinprick of potential that was starting to take hold inside my belly. I dared to hope that this tiny spot would flourish and blossom into my flesh and blood, saying a silent prayer to this babe to grow and be healthy. Hold on, my little one. What a life you shall have, how I'll love you, my sunshine!

When Ross finally left I ran into the bathroom to get the pregnancy test, waving it in front of Peter's face.

'Look, look at the two beautiful blue lines. It means I'm pregnant!'

'Pussycat, let me see—I can't believe it!' Peter said as he took me in his arms.

I got on the phone straight away to call Di, the fertility nurse from the IVF clinic, to share our surprising news. She explained that such scenarios had happened to other couples she had helped over the years, and said that while there was no scientific evidence, she believed some women's bodies just relaxed once they had a baby and they then went on to conceive a child naturally. Di also reassured me that the home kits were fairly accurate, but a blood test with my GP would make sure of the results.

I had to wait until Monday to get an appointment with my GP, so the weekend dragged on as I counted down the hours until I could get a blood test to confirm that I was pregnant. It was another day after that before a phone call finally came with the test results: I was having a baby, huzzah!

It didn't take long for Mum and my sisters to realise that something was going on. Secrets and me are not a good mix, my loud laugh and blinking eyes always giving me away. And there was nowhere to hide one bright sunny morning on the water's edge at Nielsen Park, a harbour beach in Sydney's eastern suburbs. Mum, my sister Harriet and I stood in the shallows after a swim, letting the small waves foam and crash onto our feet. The strong sunshine was drying me out, warming me up and leaving tight salty patches on my chest and arms. I winced, rubbing the stinging salt water from my eyes.

'Jessica, are you pregnant?' Mum asked out of the blue.

I said nothing, but a smile was starting to twitch at the sides of my big mouth.

'I knew it, especially when I saw your stomach today,' Harriet exclaimed. 'You can't hide anything in that leopard-print bikini of yours.'

'So that's what the two of you were whispering about when we got here!' I laughed.

They hugged me while Allegra and her two cousins rolled around like puppies, the sticky yellow sand covering their bodies. There was no pane of glass, just a big blue sky and the tide tugging at my feet as the sound of our laughter echoed off the sandstone cliffs that bookended the beach.

I had been off my medication since Allegra was around eighteen months old but I was still seeing my psychiatrist,

Dr Austin, once a month. As the pregnancy progressed I increased my appointments, sitting and talking with my doctor weekly about how I was feeling and how I wanted to future proof myself against having postnatal depression again. In the earlier appointments I had a sense that I would be okay this time, but the closer I got to my due date the more anxious I became about having PND again. It had been a year since the glass had slid away and I didn't want those scary and obsessive thoughts to sneak back into my brain again.

Dr Austin was reassuring that although I had a slightly higher chance of having PND a second time because I had already experienced it with Allegra, it was important to remind myself that the situation was very different this time. I didn't have the same stressful work conditions, plus the fact that I was already a mother meant the seismic shift that having a baby brings to one's life would not be a shock to me. And I knew to ask for help sooner if I needed it. Finally being honest with my family about the PND meant I didn't have to hide behind a mask again. They had become vigilant in checking that I was coping, something that only increased once my stomach expanded with this fresh, new chance that was growing inside of me. Rationally I knew all of this, but I was still afraid.

There was an option to go back on the medication while I was pregnant. But because I wasn't depressed there didn't seem much point in taking my trusty tablets 'just in case'. I knew how much antidepressants had helped me last time, so I could start taking them way before the dead of night started to play tricks on my mind again.

My expanding belly popped out much sooner the second time around. Once again I loved having boobs and marvelled at how my body transformed over the ensuing months.

'Mummy has a baby in there, Allegra.'

'A baby?'

'Yes, my beauty. A new little brother or sister for you.'

'Incy wincy spider climbed up the waterspout,' sang my daughter, oblivious to what having a new brother or sister might mean, and the impact it would have on her life.

Tucking Allegra into her brand new grown-up bed, she looked so small. I thought it would be a good idea to get her settled in her 'big girl' bed some time before the new baby arrived, not wanting her to feel like she had been kicked out of her cot. Peter and I made a big deal of her new room, with its brand new pale pink and blue wool rug on the floor, her vast collection of cuddly toys peeking out of four hot pink storage tubes which I had lined up opposite her bed. There was also a fluffy heart shaped pillow on her bed, resting on top of the pretty rainbow coloured sheets. Each night after I finished reading her 'just one more story', we would giggle as we lay together on her bed sharing butterfly kisses, my eyelashes fluttering on her soft cheek. When I heard her breathing deepen and slow I would lift my body as quietly as possible off her bed. Looking down at Allegra, my heart ached: she was still so small, a tiny jelly bean hidden under a doona with an explosion of pink fairies all over it. Watching while she slept, I worried how I could love another soul like I loved her. How would Allegra cope with the change to her life? How would my heart cope?

Often we would meet Harriet and her boys at the beach. Allegra and her cousins would tear around the sand while my sister and I enjoyed the sun warming our backs. Licking the drips of banana paddle-pop from my wrist, we'd sit down on our towels and watch the kids scamper at the water's edge. It was shallow and calm, so I knew I had five minutes to relax before I had to haul Allegra back onto the sand. And then another five minutes.

But there wasn't much time to take it quietly this pregnancy. During the day I was busy with Allegra and at night I would crash into bed, exhausted. Peter was still travelling for work, but when he was home on the weekends he and Allegra would have special time together. Sometimes I would get to sleep in while the pair of them snuck out of the house for hot chocolates and toasted cheese and ham croissants.

Work also continued to fill my limited time, although somewhat sporadically. My contract had expired with Seven but I was still doing some freelance shifts. Adam Boland, the creator of *Sunrise*, was very good to me and offered me fill-in newsreading shifts on the show as well as on *Weekend Sunrise*. I am forever grateful for his friendship and support. He was my professional lifeline and continued to believe in me when no one else would give me a go. I wasn't sure what would happen to my floundering career once I had my second baby. But I wasn't worried as I was determined to have a stress free pregnancy and enjoy those early days, weeks and months with my brand new baby without any added pressure or anxiety. And I would not have postnatal depression again. It would be different; it had to be different.

'Wow!' said my friend Helen, looking down at my feet.

Nooooooo! Don't look down there. I was standing in a very wet patch. My waters had just broken.

'I just love that navy blue colour on your toenails.'

I barely gave Helen a chance to finish the sentence before I fled to the door of the nail salon. Luckily the big massage chair I had been sitting in for my pedicure was made of fake black leather so it was difficult to see the damp pool of amniotic fluid I had left behind. I quickly threw some money at the woman behind the counter on the way out, telling her to keep the change. She raised her eyebrows at me and shook her head. Thank god I was wearing black leggings and a long black top. No one could see the huge damp spot on my bottom and the liquid that was trickling down the inside of my legs.

Outside the nail salon, leaning against the window of the florist next door, I managed to get my mobile out of my bottomless pit of a handbag and called the maternity ward. The midwife told me to drive straight into the hospital and that there was no time to pick up my bag from home.

I was not usually so organised, but my bag had been packed and ready as I was booked in for a caesarean in four days' time. The urgency to get to the hospital was because my baby was in the breach position, which basically meant she would be entering the world bottom first. There were extra risks that came with a natural breech delivery, for example, there is a higher chance her head could become stuck in the birth canal, depriving her of oxygen. However, my headstrong baby had other plans about the right time to make her entrance! She was not going to wait for any booked-in caesarean. She was ready and her time was now!

The midwife was worried that I might not have a lot of time before my baby was born, especially since this was my second child, and labour the second time around can be a much speedier affair. Running to the car with my toes squelching in my hot-pink thongs, I called Peter on his mobile and told him to meet me at the hospital right away. Allegra was at home with our nanny, Libby, who I rang next to explain what had happened. She told me not to worry and that she would stay with Allegra for as long as we needed.

I was surprisingly calm on the short drive to the hospital, but things became more and more uncomfortable as the familiar tug and squirm of contraction began. I reversed into the first spot I saw in the hospital car park and walked carefully inside to the lift. Pushing the up button, I bent over and leaned against the brick wall as another wave of contractions began.

'You wouldn't want to be having a baby, would you, with this lift taking so long?' joked the woman standing next to me, unaware that I was in labour. She was holding a huge bunch of pale pink roses. I simply smiled and squeezed my legs together a little tighter.

I couldn't stop kissing the forehead of my new baby girl, just minutes old. At last she was in my arms.

'I love you, I love you, I love you.'

She was bundled up tightly in a white flannelette wrap that went all the way over the top of her soft, perfect head. I held her close to my face, inhaling her sweet new smell, and covered her almond-shaped eyelids with gentle kisses.

'That's the first time she has opened her eyes,' the nurse said, as we watched her eyelids flutter open together. 'She knows her mummy's voice.'

Looking at this precious bundle, my heart expanded. There was so much room in my heart and soul for my sunshine, our new baby daughter, Giselle. I didn't want to let her go, but I had to hand her back to Peter while I was taken to the recovery ward after the caesarean. While I lay there thinking about my Giselle, the kind doctor who had delivered Allegra just over two years before came to visit me. He was reassuring and said he had the details of a midwife who could help me at home if I needed an extra pair of hands. He told me that I didn't need to go through the same situation again. He knew about my breastfeeding issues and the PND. The heavy, cold feeling of the epidural had left me numb below the waist but my heart had never felt bigger, fuller or happier. Now I had my two perfect girls, and my Petee. The regular, rhythmic sound of the beeping of monitors and machines was no match for the strong, regular beating of my heart.

The next morning I asked the midwife to open the curtains right up in my room. I wanted the blazingly bright sunlight to warm up Giselle and me; I didn't want to hide away in the dark like the last time. I was still hooked up to a morphine drip after the caesarean, so the nurse helped me get onto a walking frame and into the shower, where I sat on the plastic chair to wash my hair, my eyes and my shrunken, scarred stomach. I tried to wash my fear away too. It will be different, it will be alright, I will be able to breastfeed, I told myself.

Each time Giselle was ready for a feed I asked the lactation specialist to sit with me and watch me feed my daughter. I was determined for the experience to be different, however, when my nipples started to bleed, I recognised the tight-fisted panic in my chest. I could not let it happen again. When the tears came three days after Giselle was born, I kept reassuring myself that it was normal, just the baby blues, and it didn't necessarily mean I was heading down the postnatal depression path.

The hospital knew about my PND history and the difficulties I'd had with breastfeeding. I was also far more confident about asking for help and supervision when I needed it; I wasn't going to be pushed around by bossy midwives this time. A nurse who was regularly on the afternoon shift would come and sit with me while I fed. Still the weight of responsibility for my almond-eyed, long-lashed baby sat heavily on my chest. Although I asked the midwives to take her into the nursery at night so I could try to build up my sleep bank before we headed home, I couldn't sleep. The long burgundy curtains across my ward room windows stayed open; I had to see the shimmering lights of the city, the blinking of the planes as they took off and landed before midnight. Once the rest of the city went to sleep I stayed awake, staring at the stardust while I waited for Giselle to wake up and be brought in to me for her next feed. I wanted to stay connected to the bright world outside of my room.

'She's a hungry one, this daughter of yours,' said the snuggly midwife wheeling Giselle into my room. I couldn't stop looking at my nipples as she handed my squealing pink baby over to me.

'I don't want to keep feeding on these nipples. I am really worried it's going to get worse.'

I held my breath as I pushed down on the top of my breast with my thumb while making sure Giselle's mouth was open properly, and that her tiny tongue was in the right position.

'Ah, look at that, you're doing beautifully,' the midwife said.

'I'm not, it's hurting. It's not meant to keep hurting, is it?'

'No, it shouldn't hurt,' the midwife agreed. 'Let me have a look?'

I managed to get my thumb into Giselle's mouth, like I'd been shown by another midwife, to get her off my breast. Not surprisingly, my nipple had started to bleed. It was the same colour as my suddenly very unhappy baby girl's face.

'I am not going to keep feeding like this, I can't.'

'It's okay,' said the nurse. 'We can give her a bottle and you can give those nipples of yours a rest.'

I could have kissed that sensible midwife right on the lips.

While Giselle quietly sucked away on a bottle of formula, the midwife organised for a breast pump to be wheeled into the room. The plan was to express my milk every couple of hours to give my nipples time to recover, but also to make sure that I kept my milk supply up. As I began pumping my precious breast milk into a sterile container, the heavy blanket of night started to lift and a lilac sky gradually lightened the world outside my room. The rhythmic sound of the breast pump had sent my daughter off to sleep in the midwife's arms. I watched the pale yellow milk drip out from my nipple and politely but firmly told the midwife that this time I wasn't leaving hospital until I had the breastfeeding under control.

There would be no hiding in my room; I was determined to walk the corridors of the maternity ward pushing my baby girl in her bassinet. Her eyes still remained shut most of the time, long black eyelashes fluttering as she dreamt of life outside her cocoon. As the wheels of the bassinet bumped along the corridor, I noticed her spidery fingers poking out of the top of her wrap. Giselle had my fingers and her very own stubborn spirit.

Although Allegra liked her new tricycle, she wasn't so sure about the new sister who had taken her mummy away from her. The tricycle had been a 'present' from Giselle to her big sister. A friend had pulled a similar stunt with her kids and I thought it sounded like a good idea, a way to ease any potential jealousy and resentment about being usurped by her new baby sister. Bribery was starting early in our family.

'Shhh, Allegra . . . you don't want to wake up the other mummies who might be asleep.'

'I can't use the pedals, I can't push the pedals down. Push me, Mummy, Mummy, MUMMY!'

With one hand I bent down to push the top of the tricycle while keeping a firm hold on Giselle's bassinet with the other.

'Mummy, I'm stuck. I'm *stuck*!'

The wheels of Allegra's brand new tricycle with the silvery pink streamers were now leaving black marks on the cream skirting boards in the hospital corridor. It was impossible for me to steer the tricycle and push it and the cot all at the same time. Giselle started to cry, perhaps because we had all stopped moving. Her cries were getting louder and louder.

'Turn it off, Mummy!'

'Allegra, she is your sister, and I can't turn her off. You used to do this too, you know.'

'Put it away!'

'Don't be silly, I'm not putting your sister away. You know I love you, I will always be your mummy. I have so much room in my heart for both of you.'

'I hate you, Mummy. I don't want you to be my mummy anymore.'

Okay, so a sparkly new tricycle wasn't going to cut it; this was going to be harder than I thought. Tears started to form in my eyes. I wanted the girls to love and look after each other, be kind to one another, just like I was with my sisters. According to my mum, I loved my sisters from the start and was never jealous or asked for them to be turned off. How could I prove I was a good mummy? The most understanding, patient and clever mummy?

Once I got home with Giselle, after ten days in hospital, I made sure that I had some extra help each day. I was frightened of going back to that dark, frozen place in the weeks and months after Allegra had been born. Thankfully our nanny, Libby, was able to organise some time off from her other job so I had an extra pair of hands during the dreaded witching hours. That ugly time could strike any time from 4pm until 8pm, when everything was harder and took longer and I was at my weakest.

After a couple of weeks Libby had to return to her second job, but I still needed some help in the afternoons. Recovering from the caesarean meant I couldn't lift Allegra in and out of her highchair or bath, but what I really needed was some company during the long afternoons. Loneliness and isolation had crept up on me the last time, and I didn't want to feel marooned during the chaos of dinner, bath, breastfeeds and bedtime. My sister-in-law, whose wonderful database of contacts was matched only by her thoughtfulness, introduced me to the mother of a close friend of hers who was looking for some work. And that was how Rosa, a heavenly South American grandmother, swept into our lives with her orange lipstick, rolled Rs, embroidered pashminas and suffocatingly sweet hugs.

Rosa came over most afternoons. In theory this was to help with the girls, but what she was really doing was helping me to believe in myself. She reassured me that I was a good mother and how love was all that mattered, and she sprinkled her love throughout our house. I would take Allegra for walks to our corner deli to have some time with her while Rosa sang Spanish lullabies to Giselle before putting her down for her afternoon sleep. When we came back an hour later, the house smelt of basil, garlic and love. Allegra delighted in tasting the chunky tomato sauce that was going to be layered through the cannelloni, and slurping the minestrone soup off her Hello Kitty spoon.

Most of the time, Rosa helped bring a joy and lightness into the house that kept my monsters at bay. But I was still scared about slipping back into the dead of night fears, and already my mind occasionally played some of its terrible tricks on me. I started to have flashes of knives in my head while I held my sunny baby girl, the pane of glass that I hoped had disappeared forever sometimes propping itself up between me and the rest of the sparkling world. It wasn't always there, but at times it felt like a thick wedge of ice was stuck in my throat, choking me.

My psychiatrist helped me to understand what I was feeling. She explained that Giselle was now at a similar age as Allegra had been when my obsessive thoughts had first begun. Sometimes those feelings worked like a flashback rather than symptoms of postnatal depression. What was also very different this time around was that breastfeeding was going beautifully, no more bleeding nipples. I'd had the confidence this time to insist that the lactation expert sit with me while I fed in hospital, and I'd made a point of telling the hospital I would not be leaving until I knew that I was feeding the correct, pain-free way.

Giselle was thriving, putting on the right amount of weight and sleeping in reasonable chunks of time. I was able to sleep during those pockets of time too, and there was no anxiety or panic attacks. However, what wouldn't budge completely was that familiar, stubborn pane of glass, still separating and numbing me from the sunshine. No number of easy breastfeeds,

Spanish lullabies and caring family members would shove it completely away. A part of me felt like I had failed again because I had depression. This time I had been determined it would be different. And it was different, I was a more confident mother, but I wasn't confident that I could keep the window between me and the world open.

Each day I would get out of the house with the girls and we'd explore the streets of our neighbourhood. Those steep steps up to our front gate were not going to keep me locked away this time. Giselle was nestled snugly into my chest, strapped securely in the pink Baby Bjorn carrier that I wore like a back-pack on my front. That left my arms free to push Allegra on her tricycle, which now had a handle on the back so I could steer her along the path. With her fine blonde ponytail poking out of the back of her Tinkerbell helmet, Allegra would quickly tire of using the pedals.

'Mummy, my legs. I'm tired.'

I wasn't ready to go home—we'd only got halfway up our street. It had taken an hour for us all to get dressed and ready to get out the door. We weren't giving up yet.

'Sweet pea, stop dragging your feet along the footpath. Put them on the pedals and I can push you.' The wheels of the tri-cycle were squashing the pink bougainvillea flowers that had fallen from the tree, adding to the slimy and slippery surface.

'Darling, stay sitting on your trike. Don't stand up . . .' Just as well I'd strapped her in, making it impossible for Allegra to get out and topple the whole thing over.

'Mummy, I'm tired.'

So was I, but we still weren't going home. We managed to get to the end of the street before I agreed we could turn around. The silvery streamers from Allegra's tricycle blew back in the gentle breeze, but the fresh air wasn't enough to blow the cobwebs out of my head.

I knew I didn't need to keep struggling on my own and took my psychiatrist's advice to go back on the antidepressants. Thankfully the medication worked as effectively the second time around, and over the next couple of weeks the pane of glass gradually dissolved between myself and the rest of the world.

Riiiiiing, riiiiiiiinnnngg. What is that noise? Oh, it's the portable phone. And where is it? Not in the kitchen. Please don't let it be in Giselle's room, I'm not ready for her to wake up yet. Wait, oh yes, it's in the bathroom. I last used the phone while I was on the toilet, grabbing a moment to talk to my sister.

'Hello?' I muttered after struggling to pick the phone up from the damp sink. I suddenly heard the glamorous beeps down the line that signalled an international call.

'Pussycat, I'm in Paris. I know how much you love this city. We had dinner with the crew at Le Dôme in Montparnasse. You remember, that restaurant we went to? Where I ate two dozen oysters. And we drank too much house wine. I'm tired though. It was a long flight.'

There was silence at my end.

'Are you still there?' Peter asked.

'Yep. Wow. It sounds amazing.' My voice sounded anything but amazed. I am pissed off. 'And sorry, but I win the tired competition. Give me 24 hours on a plane, in a vacuum of peace and quiet, with no one wanting anything from me.'

Peter sensibly changed the subject. 'How are the girls? What have you been doing?'

'They're great. We went to the park.' I hate the park. 'We walked around to the shops. I got mince for dinner. Really great,' I replied.

'I miss you. Love you,' said Peter.

'Me too . . .' My voice trailed off. 'I've got to go, I can hear Giselle waking up.'

So while my husband was on the other side of the world, flying first class, eating in five-star restaurants and leading a fulfilling television career, I was back home, stifled by domesticity. My sense of self, which I had always linked to my work, had disappeared. The journalism career that I'd spent a lifetime building had vanished into the Bermuda Triangle. The phone had been very quiet, and none of my old colleagues would return my calls. I was tempted to follow Bette Davis's lead when she found herself out of work and unemployed. She took out a 'situation wanted' ad in a Hollywood newspaper: 'Mother of three—10, 11 & 15—divorcée. American. Thirty years' experience as an actress in motion pictures. Mobile still and more affable than rumor would have it. Wants steady employment in Hollywood. (Has had Broadway.)'

My ad would go something like this: 'Enthusiastic professional woman is keen for some adult conversation and me time. Has over twenty years' experience reading out loud on autocue, and most recently plenty of practice reading *We're Going on a Bear Hunt*, *Charlie and Lola* and *Spot Goes to the Park*. Loves heels, sparkles and not going to the park.'

I didn't know how much longer I could manage the girls on my own with Peter's frequent overseas travel. We would fight just before he left because neither of us wanted to be apart, and we'd fight again when he returned. I had no patience for his tiredness or jet lag. Often I would tell him to stay in a hotel to get over his travel and get rid of his bad language after being on the road with three other blokes for weeks at a time! My tiredness amplified the resentment I still had about my lack of clear career direction.

Thursday pizza nights with Georgia and her two boys kept me sane. She was also struggling with her new life. In her previous existence she had been a solicitor, and now the main topic of our conversation was toilet training and how to scrub poo off wooden floorboards. The pair of us let our kids eat their margarita pizza on the couch in front of the television while we commiserated about our lives. Laughing together while we piled four small people in the bath together helped give me the energy for another week of wiping bums, endless washing and preparing small, nutritious meals.

Although I loved being a mum, I still rebelled against what had happened to my life. It was chaotic and mundane all at once. I had never been a patient person, but now I had to focus on staying as calm as possible in the eternity it took the three of us to leave the house. We were only going to visit Mum, who lived a short drive away, but by the amount of stuff I'd packed you'd think we were travelling to Antarctica.

Allegra was onto question 251 and it was only 9am, and while concentrating on getting through the snarl of traffic on the way to Mum's place I wasn't listening properly to my daughter's latest query.

'Mummy, does Elmo have a penis?'

'Mmmm, yes,' I answered, not thinking through the consequences. Stupidly I thought this was the end of the discussion and we could move on to question 252, however, my inquisitive daughter had her follow-up question ready.

'Where is it?'

'It's hiding under his fur,' I say as authoritatively as I can manage.

Hooray, I've got through that, I think rather smugly to myself. But my satisfaction doesn't last long. On the way home from Mum's we stop off at the butcher.

'Mummy, does he have a penis?'

'Aaah, some sausages please,' I ask the butcher as my face goes the colour of Elmo's fur.

Next stop is the chemist.

'Mummy, does she have a penis?' Allegra continues her investigation.

'Umm, no,' I whisper.

'Why not?' she replies at full volume.

'Because she's a woman.'

'Women don't have penises?'

'No, we have vaginas . . .'

'What is your vagina for?' My daughter wasn't going to give up just yet. At least we had left the chemist and were back on the footpath so no one else could hear this part of the conversation. I was tempted to just ignore her. However, as we walked home, Allegra kept asking and asking. She wore me down with her persistence.

'Mmmm, your vagina is for doing wees and it's also how you were born.'

'Did I come out of your vagina?'

'Ah, yes.'

'You're joking!'

'No, my darling, I am not.' If only I had told Allegra that Elmo was a sexless Muppet! Instead I was the Muppet . . .

Every day was full of other unpredictable Elmo-like moments, but what I could count on was it all going pear-shaped every afternoon in the dreaded witching hour. Trying to single-handedly juggle dinner, bath and bed with tired babies and children meant that most afternoons I was ready to have a tantrum as well. But soon there was hope that I wouldn't always be facing the afternoons on my own when Peter was offered the news anchor position for Channel Nine's six o'clock news. The timing couldn't have been better. This was the job he had dreamt about since he was seven years old, and I had dreamt about us all living together as a family since we had our girls. It meant we could plan weekends, outings and holidays. At last his career was more family friendly.

Weekends would now see the four of us walking down our street together, Peter and I taking turns carrying Giselle or pushing Allegra in her tricycle. Now when she got tired of putting her feet on the pedals I could unstrap her and hold her soft warm hand while Peter pushed the handle on the trike.

'Family,' she said, looking up into my eyes.

'Yes, my darling, we are a family,' I replied, squeezing Peter's hand as we walked past the bougainvillea tree, ignoring the squashed dirty-pink petals on the footpath.

Eventually the phone did ring for me when the then producer of *Weekend Sunrise*, Michael Pell, asked if I could fill in on some news-reading shifts. I explained that as I was still breast-feeding Giselle she would have to come in to work with me. No problems, Michael said, and his simple answer boosted my confidence. On the weekend Peter could look after Allegra now that he was home permanently and I could leave for work. Hooray!

On my first day I put my still sleeping baby in her capsule, picked up Rosa in the dark and we drove to Martin Place in the centre of Sydney.

My friend Annebelle, who was now the head of wardrobe at Seven, had given us her office to set up in. The laminated map of Paris on her desk was the perfect place to put Giselle down for a nappy change. I left Rosa in charge while I headed downstairs to get my hair and make-up done. An hour later I was sitting on the set, having my microphone attached and joking with the hosts. As I got towards the end of my first news bulletin, I heard Giselle's cries filtering down into the studio and felt my breasts start to leak in response. Luckily I had doubled up on the pads inside my black maternity bra. After I threw to sports presenter Simon Reeve, I rushed upstairs to give Giselle a quick feed.

The four-hour weekend shift worked a treat for mother and baby, and those small steps back into the television world helped me realise that I could still do it. Even better, I was back home before lunch to spend the rest of the day with the girls and Peter. Life seemed to be settling into a happy rhythm.

Every Tuesday I'd meet Harriet and Mum at the food growers' market at Moore Park. Claudia had a stall selling her exquisite jams and chutneys so we'd drop around to see her first before I'd stock up on sugary sweet cupcakes and organic red apples. Once we had our takeaway coffees carefully balanced in hand, we would push our prams to the nearby playground. Mum would excuse herself, making no secret of the fact that she was well and truly over playgrounds, and I would cope with the slippery dip thanks to the company of my sister and sugary treats. While Giselle slept in her pram, Allegra chased around after her cousin Elliott. I was much more relaxed about Giselle falling asleep wherever she could rather than rushing home to get her into the cot, something I had been fanatical about when Allegra was the same age.

Although now I liked to focus on the light side of life, there was always a dark side lurking in the shadows. My mental health continued to be good and I was still taking my antidepressants, but I worried that this sweet spot wouldn't last for our family. I knew that life was made up of messy, inconvenient and heart-breaking matters, and despite being a grown-up my Mum's bipolar disorder could still bring me to my knees when it reared its nasty head over the years.

'Your mother has been hoarding her medication,' said the nurse at the other end of the line.

'What?'

'We found a stash in her bedside drawer. I think you'd better come in.'

'I'm on my way,' I said, my mind racing. 'I just have to drop my daughter at an appointment. I'll be there in twenty minutes.'

Mum had been in the private psychiatric hospital for ten days. She did not seem to be improving and the phone call confirmed my worries. What was she up to? I didn't have the energy for this I thought as I drove up the windy hill towards the clinic, oblivious to the glorious beach view. Usually the sight of the ocean lifted my spirits, but on that day the sea just looked angry and grey, the waves dumping surfers off their boards onto the sandbar.

'What happened?' I asked the head nurse.

'Your mother told the night nurse she had a stash of tablets and she was frightened about what she might do with them.'

'What she might do?'

'Don't worry, we took the tablets,' the nurse reassured me. 'And we've removed the sharp objects from her room.'

'Sharp objects!'

'Yes, you know how she has been doing all that sewing? Well, we've confiscated her scissors and sewing needles.'

'Can I go in and see her?'

I knocked gently on Mum's door; there was no reply but I pushed it open anyway. She was lying on her bed in the corner of her room. Her eyes seemed to have lost their light, and as I reached over to touch her hand her green eyes met mine, the same colour as my new baby's eyes. But there was no light and joy in them now. They reminded me of a shark, dead, unblinking, unable to close and switch off. I looked around the sparse pale blue room that Mum had been decorating with the colourful felt Christmas decorations she had been sewing since she was admitted to hospital.

Why, I wondered, did she always get sick before, after or during Christmas time? The months of December and January always filled my sisters and me with trepidation, wondering when the bipolar crash would hit our mother. I had long since given up on the idea of normal family holidays, despite maniacally trying to make my own little family as 'normal' as possible.

A huge stick that was propped against the windowsill caught my attention and I walked over to examine it. It hadn't been there the day before.

'I got that from the park this morning.'

'The park? Come on, Mum, you know it's not safe to wander around alone in the bushland early in the morning. Anything could happen.'

'I needed to get my coffee.'

'But the cafe is in the opposite direction, plus there's the cliffs.' I said firmly.

My eyes were suddenly drawn to the bedside table and the now empty drawer as a horrific realisation struck. 'Mum, what were you doing with those tablets?'

'I don't know.'

'You can't do that, okay?'

'I told the nurse.' She sounded contrite, like a child.

'I know, I've spoken with her.'

'I want my scissors back. I want to do my sewing.'

'No, you can't have them back yet,' I said gently. 'They're worried about you—we're all so worried about you. You have to promise me that you'll talk to me before doing something like that again. You have a daughter here who loves you, two other daughters who love you, and four grandchildren. We all love you. We need you. You can't die yet, you have to promise me.'

'I can't promise you,' said Mum, her voice trailing off into a whisper.

My mobile started to ring and I recognised the number; it was the clinic telling me I was fifteen minutes late to pick up Allegra. I had to go but I was afraid of leaving my mother alone. I had perfected the role of good daughter. That particular mask had helped me over the years when Mum's bipolar disorder landed her in hospital for long periods of time. But the mask of motherhood was a harder one for me to hide behind.

What sort of mother did I want to be? I didn't want my girls to deal with a miserable mum, to feel responsible for her happiness. I wanted to be in the moment for my daughters but my tap-dancing act of constant cheeriness didn't cut it anymore. I had been putting pressure on myself to always be upbeat with my girls, laughing, telling stories, entertaining and never sad.

That was not a realistic way to live either. Deep down I think I was afraid that if my mothering style included both light and shade, the shade would take over. Despite my medication and regular counselling appointments, I still had a habit of going privately to the worst-case scenario. I needed to remind myself that although I was like my mother in some ways, we were also very different. History was not and would not repeat itself. I had worked hard to get my head together again, I had worked hard on my marriage, and now I was working hard on being the best mother for my daughters.

But what was my insufferable optimism teaching my girls about how to regulate their emotions? I knew that life was not all about sparkles and rainbows but I wanted to protect my girls from disappointment and pain. I wanted to shower them and myself in the sequins and shimmer I had yearned for in my younger life. How could I tread that delicate path of protecting them but also preparing them for the slings and arrows of life?

Two sulphur-crested cockatoos sat on the top branch of the Moreton Bay fig, grey beaks touching and yellow crests flicking off the top of their heads. A flash of white wings appeared behind the leaves, then another flash, then another. There must have been about fifty birds high up in the boughs of the tree. Some cheeky cockies were breaking branches and pulling leaves off, spitting them onto the dirt below. The first pair I spotted turned their backs on the brand new morning, too busy squawking at one another and playing to act as lookouts for the rest of their crew.

'How much longer? Are we there yet?' Allegra sang out. I stopped gazing at the cockatoos and concentrated on finding a parking spot. I'd already done three loops around the block, and I didn't want to park illegally again. Peter was already cross that I'd got so many parking tickets.

'Mummy, I'm bored of the car, I want to get out!' Thankfully, a spot appeared close to the playground. Keeping Allegra close while I clipped eight-week-old Giselle into her Baby Bjorn carrier on the front of my chest was always a struggle, then I had to balance my large leopard-print canvas bag on my shoulder. The bag was packed with wipes, nappies, sunblock, sunhats, spare Dora the Explorer underpants, rice crackers, mini packets of apricots, and vegemite sandwiches cut into triangles then squished in plastic ziplock bags to protect them from the leaking Disney princesses water bottle.

'Wait, Allegra, hold on to Mummy's hand.'

'I want my stroller, I want to bring my dolly's stroller, Mummy. Mummy!'

'Please, Mummy, may I have my stroller is what you say, Allegra. And no, you can't, it's too hard for Mummy to get it out of the car. My hands are full.'

'Please, Mummy, please, Mummy, Mummy, Mummy!'

I could feel some other mothers' eyes on me as they walked past. Should I stay strong, for the sake of . . . what? But if I don't say no to Allegra now, will she one day become a nightmare teenager and spoilt-brat grown-up who thinks the world owes her a living?

'Mummy, I want my stroller. I want it, I want it, I want it! Please, please, pleeeease . . .'

I opened the boot and got the tiny stroller out.

'Say thank you to Mummy . . .'

Allegra had already grabbed the stroller and run off, pushing it speedily down the uneven footpath.

'Wait, wait, slow down!' I shouted, bolting after her. It's hard to keep up as my centre of gravity has shifted with Giselle strapped to my front. All I could see was the top of Giselle's white cotton hat, and her little arms and legs flapping out the sides of the bright pink carrier.

What was it about trips to the park that I still didn't like? I had hoped I would eventually come to enjoy them since I spent so much time there. Perhaps it was because my life had diminished into the minutiae of swings, slippery dips and seesaws. If only I had some regular paid work every now and then it would be perfect. My lack of confidence when I went out with Peter to his work functions continued because I had nothing to contribute to the adult conversations. I was tired of trying to explain what I was doing and not doing with my career. I filled gaps in the conversation with stories about my husband's exotic travels. It had been years since I'd been on a plane myself. I had run out of my own stories.

Instead it seemed that I had become my worst nightmare, an ungrateful, self-absorbed mother. It was clear that getting back into the paid workforce would be good for my self-esteem, and it would also give me something fresh to talk about apart from my current obsession with toilet training. Did you know it is very hard to clean poo off the bars of a cot? Did you know it can take a whole afternoon to discover your daughter has poo stuck between her toes and has been happily walking it through the house?

I liked it when Allegra stayed on the swing. That way I could strap her in and she couldn't go wandering off, and I didn't have to deal with the brawls between kids over buckets and spades in the sandpit.

'Let's count to fifty, Allegra, how about fifty more pushes on the swing?' I suggested, ignoring the little boy dressed in a blue Octonauts t-shirt who was patiently waiting for his turn. I'd successfully avoided any eye contact with his mother, whose laser-beam look said, 'For god's sake, get your daughter off the swing, it's my son's turn now.'

But my sense of fair play had long gone; I would do anything to delay our shift to the sandpit. The sand was revolting, a dirty grey colour thanks to the pesky ibises and pigeons constantly shitting in it. Already there were plenty of kids with used take-away coffee cups to scoop up the foul sand, trickling it through their sticky fingers to make poo-flavoured chocolate cakes and pies. Plus moving to the sandpit might mean I had to unstrap Giselle from my chest, and I loved keeping her close to me. It made my heart sing to put my nose to the top of her head, breathing in her very essence. I even took her sunhat off so I could cover her in kisses. Her cat-shaped eyes would light up when she spotted the grotty pigeons, and her legs kicked out in excitement at the amateur baking going on in the sandpit. Giselle kept me grounded and earthed when I felt like escaping my life. But Allegra was ready to run to the sandpit, and she was desperately trying to slide herself under the safety chain that had kept her in place on the swing.

'Okay, just a sec, let Mummy do it,' I said, as she tried to wriggle away.

'The sandpit, Mummy. Let's make cakes in the sandpit.'

'I know, how about we play shops in the cubby house, right next to the sandpit? That will be much more fun. You could be the shopkeeper and I can buy the cakes from you,' I suggested in desperation.

'No, I want to make a black forest cake in the sandpit.'

'Okay,' I replied, defeated.

While I fashioned cherries and cream out of the grey sand, I wondered why the sight of all this equipment and activity makes me feel so despondent? There were only so many times I could push the swing, stand at the bottom of the hot slide looking enthusiastic, and then stand under the ladder ready to catch any wobbly legs missing their footing as they climbed to the top of the pirate ship. Once was never enough, it was always again, again, again, Mummy. More, Mummy—please, let's do it again.

I was dragged from my self-absorbed ponderings by the sound of Allegra's voice, screaming from the top of the slippery dip.

At least she was out of the grotty sandpit but I didn't like what I was hearing from the play equipment.

'Go away, everybody. *My* slippery dip. I'm not sharing. Go *away*!'

It sounded like good advice: all I wanted was to go away and hide while the line of kids waiting to use the slippery dip grew. But my daughter wasn't budging. Her strong, defiant nature might one day be a trait worth celebrating when she was older, but why couldn't she be a little easier and more easy going now? Why couldn't her mum be more patient and content too? Why did I feel like I was no good at this mothering caper?

'Come on, darling, down you get. Look at the other girls and boys, they're waiting their turn. Come on, time to slide down. Remember, caring is sharing,' I sang through a fake smile. My words were probably more for the benefit of the expensively clad mother standing smugly near the cubby house than my single-minded daughter. Eventually, I managed to drag Allegra down the slide while keeping mainly upright with Giselle strapped again to my front.

A sick feeling was starting in my stomach and I knew that our exit from the park was coming, and fast. Was I the only mum who had a child who screams, rants and raves? Ironically, only two hours before a paparazzi photographer had captured a picture of us laughing together. I had my black fifties-style sunnies on, a pink top and denim shorts. Giselle was asleep, nestled into my chest, and Allegra was grinning and looked like the sort of girl who would share. Don't be fooled by such images; pretty soon it all ends in tears, for everyone.

'Sit in your seat. Let me strap you in.' I heard the panic rising, my voice thin and shrill. I managed to get Giselle clipped into her baby capsule, but Allegra was kicking the window and screaming so I couldn't get the three-way clips into the buckle of her car seat. I was sweaty and my fingers were stinging from where my eldest daughter had kicked them, determined not to stay in her car seat.

'Stop it now! Do not kick me! *Stop!*' I had totally lost it, bellowing in a she-wolf voice that I had never heard before. The windows of the car were steamed up, with little footprints marking the glass. Finally clipping the buckle in, I sat back in my seat and started to quietly cry. My eldest daughter and I were both railing against the world and the unfairness of it. For Allegra, it was unfair because she had to be strapped into her seat and leave the park. And for her mum, it was unfair because I was being undone by a simple outing to the park.

I started the engine and cranked up the air conditioning to demist the windows and cool down. My hands were on the steering wheel but we were not going anywhere. Giselle had gone to sleep, oblivious to the hot, melting, messy pile of rage in the car. I would sit there until the screaming and kicking stopped.

'Where are you, Mummy?' Allegra called.

'Upstairs!'

'Where?'

'On the toilet,' I called back.

'*Where?*'

'On the *toilet*!'

'I love you, Mummy. I *love* you, Mummy!'

Allegra was suddenly bounding on the stairs, her little sister trailing after her. Giselle was shuffling down the stairs on her bottom, she never crawled in the usual way, but managed to move around very efficiently! Her Barbie Mariposa was in one hand while she slid along the smooth floorboards happy to entertain herself. Allegra continued talking as she walked up to me where I was perched on the toilet.

'A wee or a poo?' she asked.

'A poo.'

'Will it be a long time or a short time?'

'Not too long—just give me a minute.'

The inquest continued. 'You've got a tampon.'

'Yes.'

'You've got your period.'

'Yes.'

'When will I have my period?' asks my three-and-a-half-year-old.

'When you're older.'

'When's that?'

'Ahhh . . .'

Lightning fast, Allegra changes tack. 'Do you know that Daddy says "shut up" and "fuck"?'

I know what I want to say, but I stay quiet as I dry my hands on the towel.

'How about steak and corn for dinner tonight?'

'Does that mean the smoke alarm will go off again?' asks Allegra.

'Mmm, not necessarily . . .'

Cooking had never been high on my list of talents. To be honest, I was a crap housewife and was still fighting against the machine of routine, folded clothes and having a place for everything.

'Why do we have so much clutter?' Peter would ask as he tripped over backpacks, shoes and puzzle pieces. 'I bet other people don't live like this.' Even though our long-suffering cleaner, Christina, still came once a week, I couldn't keep the house tidy. There were explosions of pipe-cleaners, glitter, Barbie shoes, rainbow-striped teddy bears and Strawberry Shortcake dolls scattered in every corner of the house. Hiding under our king-size bed were dusty dummies and plates of green cut-up apple that had shrivelled to look like wrinkled prunes, porous with mould. The dirty dishes would pile up in the sink after the effort of cooking dinner and getting the girls to bed had taken all of my stamina. Those plates could wait, and I knew Peter was good at washing up. He is one of those kind souls who cleans up and wipes the bench tops before the cleaner arrives, so the house wasn't a total shambles.

Our study slash junk room door was permanently closed, with a note on it asking Christina not to bother. The room had become a burial ground for files, old toys and boxes that hadn't been unpacked since we moved in three years before. The cupboard under the stairs was jammed full, and if you opened the door, plastic bags, umbrellas, containers of play dough and Christmas decorations tumbled out. Didn't other women have piles of stuff everywhere? Surely just folding the clothes was enough effort? Wobbly stacks of pink t-shirts, stripey leggings, tutus, my granny whacker underpants, and Peter's giant navy polo shirts and extra-large beige shorts remained at the bottom of the stairs.

Sick of always putting them away, I set myself a challenge: how long would they stay there for? Would they magically transport themselves to the top of the stairs? I was hoping Peter would see them and put them in the drawers. His excuse was that he didn't know where the girls' clothes went and it was best to leave it for me. 'Anyway,' he said, 'I do the garbage. That's my job.' Ten days was the record time the piles of clothes stayed on the bottom step until I cracked and put them away myself. Huffing and puffing, I crammed them into drawers already bursting with clothes.

Visiting the immaculate homes of friends left me feeling inadequate. How did they do it? Where did they stuff their mess? Surely I wasn't the only one living in a permanent state of camouflaged chaos? I reminded myself of the words of Rosa, the South American grandmother who rescued me in the days after I brought Giselle home. She told me that a home was a place that you lived in, not a showroom. But I remained envious of other people's ability to be organised and tidy. Why couldn't I be like that too?

CHAPTER TWELVE

The day Mum went missing began much like any other day. I was hurling clothes out of the 'clean' laundry basket as I tried to find Allegra's favourite t-shirt.

'Yes, I know, it's the one with the black poodle on the front with red bows on the ears. And yes, it's got long red sleeves. I know you want to wear it. And yes, Mummy is looking for it.'

'Mummmmmy, I have to wear that top!'

'Oh look, I found it—um, but it looks like there's some bolognese on it from dinner last night.'

'But I want to wear it!' Allegra wailed.

'Okay, but we have to get dressed *now*. Arms up above your head.'

If I squinted I couldn't really see the grubby red marks splattered over the front of the t-shirt. However, no amount of squinting stopped me seeing the pyjama pants that remained firmly on her bottom half. Blue and covered in cranes and bull-dozers, they were the current clothing favourite on loan from her cousin Elliot. The outfit was finished off with white gumboots dotted with red and green stars.

'Terrific,' I said.

'Mummy, can I watch a *Charlie and Lola* now, the one about the guinea pig?'

'What do you say?' I prompted.

'My royal servant.'

'Excuse me, I am not your royal servant!' I had to smile though, given I often felt like the domestic help in our house. But it also made me feel guilty that the girls were watching too many Barbie DVDs; those princess, fairy and musketeer Barbies all had royal servants.

'Alright, just one episode.' Yet again my well-intentioned 'no television in the mornings' rule had lasted all of an hour.

While the telly blared away, I hid the laundry basket in the study. I'd work out whether they were clean or dirty clothes another day, or year. My daughters' drawers were full of pretty dresses but Allegra insisted that these nice new clothes were too scratchy, itchy, lacy and boring. But I refused to give them away because of the exorbitant price I'd paid for them. And I hoped that Giselle would wear her big sister's clothes when she grew into them.

I'm like a magpie—drawn to sparkles, colour and shiny things. I like to stock my nest, and that of my daughters, with as much colour and twinkle as possible. Clothes have a transformative power for me, and I love to put on a different 'costume' depending on my mood. It's my protection, my armour against the day. It's something my dear husband doesn't get, nor does he understand my desire to stuff the wardrobe with more floral pants, jumpsuits, boots and sequin dresses.

'How many more Collette Dinnigan dresses do you need?' Peter would ask.

I run through my list of justifications. It was on sale. It's not new, I've had it for ages. Oh there's nothing in the bag, it's empty. I work hard and I wanted to reward myself. I don't really have that many frocks. I will have these gowns forever, it's an investment—the girls will even wear them as vintage clothing one day. Really it's a bargain, if you think about how much wear the dresses will get.

Besides, anyone who doesn't realise a shoe can change your life hasn't heard of Cinderella!

On that particular morning I went for a short purple-flowered dress teamed with flat studded ankle boots. It was a look inspired by a photo I saw of supermodel Kate Moss in one of those fun trashy magazines. I was a late adopter of the trend but I wanted to feel a bit hip, even if my life was anything but that at the moment. Given my fashion obsession, it was no surprise that my girls were also attached to their 'looks', even if that look said 'I've just rummaged through the charity clothing bin and nobody cares for me, or even brushes my hair'. I didn't have the energy today to argue, cajole or bribe my daughters with freckles and gummy bears. They looked like a pair of wild waifs but it was not a battle worth fighting, even if the other mums at day care had tidy children and didn't look sweaty and worn-out when they dropped their kids off.

'Breathe in, breathe out, breathe in,' I kept telling myself while trying to ignore the tussle over who owned the Little Miss Giggles water bottle. I was about to lose it with both of my little misses, but I tried to remember the calm voice of my counsellor and to repeat those breathing techniques she had suggested. I was also still seeing my psychiatrist but only twice a year to check on my medication. My antidepressants were very useful for keeping myself on an even keel, but strategies like these also helped to stop myself from being overwhelmed by the panic and chaos of the morning. I reminded myself that having knotty hair wouldn't scar my daughters for life. Or would it? I remembered that Mum used to send us to school with knots, and I still worried too much about what others thought of me. Perhaps that's because some people remembered my face from television and that made me feel more visible, especially when one of my daughters was having a meltdown in the supermarket because they couldn't have the supersized Cherry Ripe stacked right in front of them.

At age two and a half, Giselle was going through her Disney princess phase and her current muse was Rapunzel, the damsel with long, tangle-free hair and a purple polyester gown. Despite the sticky, humid day, my baby girl was very happy to put on this scratchy-looking dress.

'Mumma, the sleeves,' she said, holding her arms up.

'Perfect, they're just perfect,' I replied.

'Nooooo, not long enough. They have to go down to here,' she said, indicating her fingers.

'They do go down to there. They are long sleeves. It's a long-sleeved dress. But if you bend your elbow they will creep up a bit,' I explained.

'They have to be *long*!'

'They are long,' I said, trying to sound convincing.

What was I doing, arguing the merits of the sleeve length of Rapunzel's costume with a two-and-a-half-year-old girl? I would agree to almost anything to get the girls out the door so I could see Mum before hospital visiting hours were over. But it was like herding cats, although our cats Alfie and Vanessa (Audrey had recently died after a long and happy life!) were more obedient. I was ready for a big strong gin and tonic and a lie down and it was only eight o'clock in the morning. Instead, I focused firmly on holding miss poodle top by the hand while carrying the princess of the not-long-enough sleeves on my hip.

It was a hot and sweaty day, and it was only getting stickier as I tried to steer my eldest daughter away from the dog poo that she seemed magnetically attracted to on the footpath. We finally arrived at day care.

Buzzzzzzzzzzzzzzzzzzzzzzzz.

'Allegra, stop pushing the button. I'm sure the teachers know we're here,' I said, kicking the gate open with my boot. As we manoeuvred through the entrance, I realised my dress was feeling a bit tight and uncomfortable. A quick readjustment revealed why: it was caught up in my knickers. I'd just bared my bottom to the world. At least I was wearing my granny whackers, comfy, bottom-covering, man-repelling underpants that had replaced the Simone Péréle lace G-strings I used to regularly buy from the third floor of David Jones. That fine, delicate lingerie was now shoved to the back of my top drawer somewhere, rolled up and forgotten like that part of my life.

'Mummy, have you got my water bottle? Where's my hat?' Allegra demanded.

'Um, your hat is in the bottom of your Dora bag. And your water bottle is where it always is, in the side pocket of your bag.'

Despite all these challenges in coming to terms with being a mother, I had always regarded myself as a five-star daughter. Mum's latest hospital admission came only eight months after she had last been in the psych ward and hoarding her medication. My days were again dominated with day care drop-off and then daily visits to Mum in the psychiatric hospital. Mum had been going downhill after her latest bipolar episode, and I desperately hoped this most recent spell in hospital would give her doctors a chance to fine-tune her medication, keep an eye on her, and stop her from slipping into that scary, black cave of nothingness. My sisters and I tend to go into paramedic mode when Mum gets sick, but despite our years of experience dealing with Mum's illness, our ability to handle different situations was still erratic. Even though we had spent far too many hours talking to doctors and hospital administrators over the years, each time Mum disappeared into her mad, bad headspace, I still felt vulnerable and frightened. Just like the little girl I was when she first became sick.

'Hey, aren't you that news lady?' the man behind the coffee counter asked.

'That's me,' I smiled while gritting my teeth, thinking, please don't ask me anything else. 'Can I have a skim cappuccino, a babycino, and a nice and hot but not too frothy flat white, please?'

Mum liked her coffee hot. Sometimes a good caffeine fix had been enough to elicit a sliver of a smile from her during hospital visits. I found myself feeling desperately optimistic as I balanced a tray of takeaway coffees in one hand and held Giselle's hand with the other while we walked towards Mum's room. Was it a mistake to bring my baby into a place like this? I figured that it was life, both a part of our life now and part of my earlier life. Plus I believed the combination of a coffee and cuddle from both of us might help Mum. I wanted Mum to know how loved she was, and there were two generations of girls who would not give up on her.

But Mum was not in her room. Her bed was empty and the staff had no idea where she had gone.

'What do you mean she's not here?' I said to the nurse on duty.

'Well, she seemed a bit upset this morning when we told her she would be changing rooms. And then when we went to check on her a little later, she wasn't in her bed,' the nurse said, sounding as if this type of missing patient scenario was routine.

'Where is she? How could she have just walked out of here and disappeared?' I asked, trying to keep calm.

'We don't know.'

'How can you not know? You are here at the desk. How can she walk past without anybody noticing?'

'I'm sure she will be back soon.'

'And if she's not?'

'We'll have to call the police.'

There had been plenty of times when I had been worried about what Mum might do, but this time I was really scared. I searched her room. Her wallet was there but she had taken her mobile. I grabbed my phone out of my bag and called her, but it went straight through to her voicemail. I waited for the beep and left as calm a message as I could manage. 'Mummo, it's me. Remember we were coming to see you this morning? I've got coffee. We will wait here for you.' Then I sent her a text message: *Mummo, where are you? I'm here with Giselle. Please let me know you're okay.*

I couldn't let my fear show with my little daughter by my side. I dropped the takeaway coffees in the bin and rang my sister Harriet. She was planning on meeting us at the hospital with her little boy Elliott, owner of the blue pyjama pants that my eldest daughter was currently starring in at day care.

'I'm here at the hospital but Mum's not here. She's missing,' I said.

'Missing? How can she just go missing? I thought they were meant to be keeping an eye on her,' my sister exclaimed. This sudden change of events didn't fit with her rational approach to everything.

We decided to meet at the adjoining cafe and come up with a plan. What sort of plan do you make when your mother goes missing? Caffeine seemed to be a good place to start, especially since I had tipped my latest fix in the hospital bin. I ordered some more coffees and pretended not to hear the barista joking about how much we must like his coffee.

When Harriet arrived we bribed the little people with apple juice and gingerbread men to get a few moments of peace so we could talk.

'Bang, crash, bang, crash, bang,' my daughter sang exuberantly, whacking her juice bottle on the table.

'Surely she hasn't got too far. Mum hasn't got a car,' my sister reasoned. Our conversation was being accompanied by the constant bang song from Giselle.

'Will you get that child to be quiet?' a woman yelled from the counter as she waited for her order. Most of the time I'm a polite and pleasant person, almost to the point of irritation. However, my good manners deserted me at that moment.

'I'm doing my best,' I yelled back. Harriet and I kept ignoring Giselle's 'song' while we decided to have our own search party for Mum. Then as we got up to leave the cafe I walked over to the woman and said in a cold and bitchy voice, 'I hope you ruin someone else's day. You have no idea what is happening in peoples' lives.' What I said was so out of character for me but I was finding it almost impossible not to be hysterical about what Mum had done. I almost wished I had long hair to flick over my shoulder as my tone-deaf toddler and I stumbled out. Ms Judgemental couldn't see the tears running down my cheeks.

Thankfully, today my daughter was happy to be strapped into her car seat, ready to sing along to yet another round of nursery rhymes on the CD player. I glanced in the rear-vision mirror as she made the actions to go with 'Twinkle Twinkle Little Star', grateful that she was oblivious to the unfolding family crisis.

I got on the phone. 'Petee, it's me, I'm worried about Mum,' I said, unable to articulate the details properly.

'What's happened?' he said impatiently. 'I'm about to do a news update.'

'She's gone missing. I need your help.' All the calm had disappeared from my voice.

Peter didn't miss a beat. 'Are you at the hospital? Wait there, I'm on my way.'

My husband, sister and I made an unlikely convoy, trawling the streets of the leafy well-to-do neighbourhood looking for a runaway mother. The hospital told us she'd been wearing a pink kaftan top with white pants, so I kept a lookout for a flash of pink as we drove. Thinking of that colour helped me stay in the present; I would not let my mind leap into panic mode. One steep street led to a ferry wharf that on any other day I would have thought was a beautiful spot to look out across Sydney Harbour, but today the deep blue water just frightened me. Don't let your ugly imagination go there, I thought. Then I prayed, something I had not done in a long time. The last time I had properly prayed I'd begged the god, goddess or unicorn of the holy spirit to nourish the microscopic embryo that was implanted inside me. Now I was begging the universe to keep another fragile soul alive.

Please God, let Mum be okay. Please God, don't let her die. God, stop her from hurting herself. A small voice interrupted my muddled prayer.

'Mumma, what we doing?'

'Ah, we're on an adventure.' Yeah right, some adventure, I thought. 'Daddy and your Aunty Lade and Yel are all having a drive in our cars. They're going to meet us here.'

It didn't take long for the others to arrive at the ferry wharf. While the children ran around on the grass nearby, we tried to work out what to do next.

'Do you think your mum could have got on the ferry?' Peter asked.

I looked up the ferries number on my phone and gave a garbled explanation to the woman who answered the call. 'We can't find our mum. She's missing, she managed to get out of her psychiatric hospital. And she . . .' Before I could finish, the measured voice on the other end of the line told me she would put me through to the ferry control room. My call was transferred, and this time a man answered. Gently he asked me to describe what Mum was wearing when she was last seen.

'Pink. A pink top,' I said.

I repeated the information about her leaving the hospital and gave him the address of the wharf we were standing on. He told me he would put a call through to all the ferries on the waterways, give them Mum's description and call me right back. Fifteen minutes later my mobile rang.

'We've found her,' he said.

'They've found her!' I yelled to Peter and my sister, who were keeping an eye on the kids somersaulting on the grass.

'Oh my god, is she okay?' I asked the man, silently thanking the goddess and unicorn and everyone else.

'She's sitting quietly, gazing out the window. The crew haven't said anything to her. We don't want to frighten her or cause her to do anything unexpected. Now we're going to divert the ferry to where you are,' he said.

'Thank you, thank you so much for your help, oh it means so much to us, thank you,' I babbled.

'Darlin', it's our job. Pleased we found her.'

It was going to take a while for the ferry to return, so Peter headed back to work, back to the serious business of news and tragedies happening to somebody else's family. My sister and I took the kids to wait for Mum under the shade of the ferry shelter. Stuck along the top of the wooden walls was information about ferry tickets, ads for the latest way to blast flab away from your stomach, plus some pictures of seahorses and fish found in the water nearby. We chattered about sea creatures and made some half-heartened attempts to sing silly songs about them to distract the kids. The relief and let-down of adrenaline made us light-headed and giggly. I felt drunk with relief, and wasn't sure if I wanted to yell at Mum or give her a hug when I saw her.

Suddenly I could see a ferry heading to the wharf. I told my sister to stay in the shade with the children and seahorses and I would hop onto the boat to get Mum. As it pulled up, one of the crew helped me aboard.

'I haven't told your mum that you're here. She's just through there.' He gestured through the glass doors of the ferry, pointing to the row of seats along the window.

I tried to look confident as I pulled open the door and walked across to the window seats. Ignoring the curious looks from other passengers wondering about the unexpected detour of their ferry route, I walked up to my mother. She was slumped against the window, her eyes looking desolately across the harbour and cityscape. When I reached out to touch her shoulder, she turned around and screamed in fright.

'Mum, it's okay, it's me, Jessica. Your daughter. I'm here to get you. Let's get off,' I said.

'No, no, *no*! I'm staying here—this ferry is going to Circular Quay. I'm not getting off until we get to the city.'

'Come on, it's time to go. Let's hop off here together.' I found myself taking the same tone I used to cajole my daughters into doing something they didn't want to do.

'No,' Mum said.

'Alright, I'll sit here with you and we'll get off at the Quay together.'

'No, go away, go *away*!' Mum said. She wouldn't look at me.

'I'm not going away. I am not going anywhere. Harriet and the kids are waiting for you on the wharf,' I said.

'What? What are they doing here? They shouldn't be here. I don't want to see them.'

'Come on, Mum, let's go.'

Then I just stood there; I had run out of things to say. This woman with the mad eyes wasn't my mum, not the mum I knew. Begrudgingly she got up, but brushed my upturned hand away.

'The only reason I'm getting off is because I don't want to hold up all the other passengers,' she said. Refusing to look at me, Mum staggered towards the ferry exit. I hovered right behind her, willing myself to focus on her fuchsia kaftan and not make eye contact with any other passengers.

'Thank you so much for helping us,' I said to the ferry hand, as he slid the gangplank across so we could step onto the wharf. I tried to take Mum's arm to help her, but she pushed it away. She was unsteady on her feet, a side-effect from the heavy doses of medication. Mum tried to shove past me, but I put my hand on her shoulder as she walked past my sister and her grandchildren. Their little faces were full of confusion, as just moments before they had rushed up to give their beloved grandmother a cuddle. I did my best reassuring smile and told Giselle to stay there with her aunty and cousin.

'Just hold your Aunty Lade's hand. Marmi will be okay. I've just got to take her back to the hospital. I'll see you in a minute,' I said. My sunglasses were firmly in place so my daughter couldn't see my tears.

Mum and I kept walking but somehow I managed to manoeuvre her in the direction of my car. I told her to get in, unsure what I would do if she refused to obey. Thankfully she got into the front seat without a word; I reached across her lap to clip her seatbelt in.

'Mum, we were so worried about you. We love you. We want to help you,' I said.

'I can't talk to you. I'm so angry,' she said as tears streamed down her face but still not turning to look at me.

'We love you. It's okay. It's okay,' I said. The drive back up the hill to the hospital took only a few minutes.

'Stay here, you are not coming in. I can go in myself,' she said when we arrived.

'No, I'm not dropping you off here. I am walking in with you,' I said firmly.

Yet again she shoved my hand away and shuffled up to the hospital doors, with me tagging close behind. When we reached the nurses' station in the ward she flopped down in one of the blue vinyl chairs.

'Just leave me here!' she screamed. 'Go away!'

'I'm not going anywhere. I want to make sure you are safe in your room—we don't want you disappearing again.'

Thankfully, a nurse intervened. 'It's alright, I'll take you to your room.'

'I'm coming too, Mum,' I insisted, following dutifully behind. My brave face was back in place to deal with whatever came next. But all I could think about was getting Mum settled and safe in her room.

That night as I snuggled with my girls in their beds before kissing them goodnight, my mind whirred with the craziness of the day. Our nightly routine was to lie down in the dark together and whisper about the happiest parts of their day. On this night I made a silent promise to shield them from my pain and worry. I wanted to protect them from the chaos of my childhood, and I wanted to be a perfect, happy mother. I shifted White Owlie and Rapunzel doll to the other side of the bed so I could give Giselle a proper hug. She wasn't yet three and I found the bluntness that came with such an age refreshing.

'You're hot, Mummy,' said Giselle.

'Oh, sorry . . .'

'Take the doona off. I'm hot.'

'When is it my turn?' asked Allegra.

'Five minutes.'

'Is it a long five minutes or a short five minutes?'

'Long,' said Giselle.

'When is it my turn?' Allegra asked again.

'Soon.'

'How soon?'

'Soonish.'

'But how long is soon?'

'Now. I'm coming now.'

'Come closer, Mummy,' Allegra said, patting her princess pillowcase. I had just spent two hundred dollars at the hairdresser getting them to comb the nits out of her hair. Expensive but worth it because it short circuited the merry-go-round of nit infestation that seemed to last for months. I didn't want to get too close, even though I was already scratching my scalp at the thought of the creepy crawlies.

'Put your head here. Speak in a louder voice,' Allegra instructed.

'How's this? Can you hear me?'

'Yes. That's good. Where do you go when you die, Mummy?'

If I stayed quiet, lying there under the Disney Princess doona, maybe Allegra would ask a different question. Giselle called out from her bed. 'Die? Did Allegra say die? What's that?'

'I'm worried about dying. I don't want you and Daddy to die and leave me alone,' Allegra said.

'I won't leave you alone.'

'But will you die?'

'We all die, but not for a very long time.' I crossed my fingers.

'What's heaven, Mummy?'

'It's a place where you feel the happiest. Everything that makes your heart sing will be there.'

'Promise me you'll never die.'

I stayed silent.

'When I die, promise me you'll lie here with me always and never leave.'

Then I stroked her hair until she fell asleep. Giselle was already dancing in her dreams. My mum used to pat my head to help me fall asleep. It made me feel safe. Loved.

CHAPTER THIRTEEN

'Red, and yellow and pink and green, purple and orange and bluuuue. I can sing a raaaaainbow, sing a raaaaainbow . . .'

'Stop it, I don't like it,' Allegra complained.

'How about this one? The dinosaurs were dancing round the prehistoric swamp, they shook their heads, swished their tails, and . . .'

'No more singing, Mummy,' my three-year-old Giselle said bluntly.

I was still struggling to get regular television work. The occasional fill-in news presenting on *Weekend Sunrise* wasn't enough to restore my confidence. Although I wanted to move on from my very public professional fall from grace, it still dragged me down. I had to come up with something drastic. What were my talents? Hey, I play dress-ups and sing with my girls, so I could work as a presenter on *Play School*, the long-running children's show on the ABC, right? Of course—that's what any tone-deaf person would think would be a good career option. At least I hadn't forgotten to jump in the deep end and take a risk.

With my daughters pretending to be mermaids wearing their green Princess Ariel tails in the bath, I gave them a concert of the songs I had to perform for my audition. I needed all the practice I could get. And as I knew those tails meant they couldn't get out of the bath in a hurry, I had a captive audience.

After numerous phone calls to the executive producer's office, my persistence had finally paid off and I had been given a break, an audition on *Play School*. I thought a job starring in a children's television show would solve all my problems: I would have a title, a purpose, and something to tell the car parking attendant and the butcher.

And that was how I found myself having an out-of-body experience in one of the vast ABC television studios at Ultimo in Sydney.

'The dinosaurs were dancing round the prehistoric swamp, they shook their heads, swished their tails,' I sang, valiantly wiggling my bottom at the camera crew filming my audition.

The pianist with his long groovy hair pulled back into a ponytail looked like a frustrated musician who had no time for impostors like me. Determined to ignore his 'too cool for school' vibes, I warbled on through 'Sing a Rainbow', a song with far too many key changes for an amateur like me. That part of the audition finally ended as I attempted to trace the shape of a rainbow in a jumble of hand movements.

For years as a news presenter, I had been paid to read out loud for a living. How hard could it be to tell a kids' story? I told stories to my girls all the time. All of my enthusiasm, energy, frustration and desperation went into the story of the dinosaur who stomped through the forest. I leapt through the air, raised my eyebrows and made spectacular sound effects.

I floated above the cavernous television studio and spotted the real stars of the show, the toys: Big Ted, Little Ted, Jemima and Humpty Dumpty. If someone happened to look through the huge glass windows that surrounded the room, they would be convinced the woman in the red t-shirt, jeans and sneakers had lost her mind. My dinosaur tale was the performance of a lifetime, but instead of applause there was just silence—an awfully long silence.

'Aaaah, ummm, you are definitely an enthusiastic storyteller,' said the director. I looked at her expectantly, convinced she would offer me the job on the spot.

'Okay then, thank you,' she said, while one of the cameramen held open the studio door for me to exit.

Not surprisingly, the powers that be at the ABC didn't like it either.

But I wasn't giving up yet. Realising I needed professional help, I enlisted the expertise of *Play School* royalty, my friend Jay Laga'aia, who listened patiently while I read him some kids' stories. Jay told me to lose the newsreader precision and perform like I was simply talking to my daughters. Next he played some songs on his piano while he heard me 'sing'. The sounds coming out of my mouth weren't even close to the notes, but Jay was still encouraging and gave me the number of a fabulous singing teacher. My desire to crack the nursery rhyme code led to the beginning of a surprising and special friendship when my singing teacher, Margi, helped me get in tune with myself. It wasn't about hitting the right notes—my renditions of 'Little Peter Rabbit' and 'Sing a Rainbow' were still all over the place—it was about finding my confidence again. That unfamiliar sense of contentment sat happily inside my chest as I stood in Margi's small front room, singing to her black cat, Carlotta, curled on top of the piano.

'Doe rayyyy, meee, faaaaarrrr, soooooo, larrrrrrrr, teeeeeeee,' I sang.

'Again, listen to me,' Margi said. 'Do, re, mi, fa, so, la, ti. Try it again and imagine you're singing straight through the window, out into those trees.'

'Do, rayyyy, mee, farrrrrr, soooo, larrrrr, teeeeee,' I sang again, as Carlotta flicked her black tail.

I gradually found my equilibrium in those weekly lessons. That hour each week was my time, my bubble, just for me. In Margi's little room I was just Jessica, stripped bare and unplugged. There was no one there to judge, snigger or criticise me, so I let the notes, rhymes and vibrations caress me. Singing scales, flubbering my lips, and blowing fart sounds while making a cat's bum face brought me simple joy, something that had been missing since I lost my high-profile co-hosting gig on *Today*. Although I had my girls and my Petee, there was still a part of me that felt a failure. The technicolour notes of 'Sing a Rainbow' were helping to mend the part that still thought it was not good enough. I knew I had to find joy in my professional life again and to work with people who made me feel good, not people who made me second-guess every word, sentence and loud laugh.

Finally I got a second crack at *Play School*. Jay went over the moves I needed, coaching me through the steps known as the grapevine. My singing teacher got me as close to the right notes as I was ever going to be. This time there was no out-of-body experience as I shook my head and wiggled my tail for the director; even my dinosaur drawing wasn't too bad. I finished the audition, knowing there was nothing more

I could have done. The phone call came a few weeks later, but unfortunately I still wasn't quite good enough. I sulked for a few days but kept drawing a blank on how I could reinvent myself.

My cars tyres crunched on the wet, gravelly road. Or maybe not—it was hard to hear anything over my daughter's screams.

'I don't want to go to the party! Don't make me go, Mummy. I don't want to go!'

'Come on, let's give it a go. Draw on the bravery and courage that I know is inside of you. You know, Mummy still gets shy. I don't like walking into a room full of people. I'm nervous too.' Then I noticed that my car's parking sensors were suddenly going nuts.

Beep, beeeep, beeeeeeeeeeeep.

'I am not going!' Allegra yelled, oblivious to the fact that our car was now jammed between two other vehicles. My attempt at a U-turn to grab the only free spot on the narrow street on this wet Saturday morning hadn't gone well, and now I knew what the crunching noise was. There was a large dent in the side of the expensive sedan I had reversed into because I hadn't turned the wheel far enough to clear the car on the other side of the road. We were already an hour late for the birthday party. The mermaid-themed event was Allegra's first party invitation since starting at big school, so I wanted to make an effort to get her there. Why was I letting a six-year-old's birthday party freak me out?

Allegra's litany of excuses for not getting out of the car was relentless from the backseat. Bribery was the only way we were going to get to this party. I had already bribed myself with a new purchase, the brown and black sequinned handbag that was lying beside me on the passenger seat.

'We don't have to stay long. Let's just go and have a look. And if you do that we'll go and get hot chips afterwards,' I said. The sound of my cheery voice with its upward inflection even irritated me.

'Sooooooo, I only need to have a quick look,' Allegra said. She was already a skilled negotiator at just five years of age.

'Yes,' I said, trying not to look at the dented panel door of the car as we crossed the road to the party. Although I was tempted to drive away to the safety of home, leaving the damage and anxiety behind, I was not going to give up just yet. I sifted through layer upon layer of junk on the floor of the car, trying to find a scrap of paper and a pen to place a note on the windscreen of the European car I'd left quite an impression on. The task reminded me of an archaeological dig: forget carbon dating, I could recount my entire week by what I excavated from inside my car. Pink ballet slippers, a pink lunchbox, a purple fairy wand, scraps of popcorn stuck to the carpet, polka-dotted tap shoes, takeaway coffee cups, one pussycat gumboot, Mac lipsticks, tweezers, green nail polish, shredded polystyrene (from a snow storm in the backseat when stuck in traffic on Wednesday), a yellow school hat, a library bag, a black cocktail dress still covered in plastic from the dry cleaner, and a nit-infested pale pink Mason Pearson hairbrush. But there was no paper or a pen. I ripped the party invitation in half and used a half-melted orange lip liner that I found in the glove box to scribble down an apology and my mobile number. Slipping the torn note under the damaged car's windscreen wiper, my daughter took a vice-like grip on my jeans.

The pair of us walked tentatively towards the house with the pink and white balloons tied to the front gate.

'Come in, come in, the girls are downstairs, Allegra,' said the mother who was hosting the party.

'Mummy, come with me,' Allegra implored, her little fingers digging tightly into my legs.

'I'm coming, I won't leave you.'

Downstairs, a pretty twenty-something mermaid in a long red wig, glittering blue singlet and shimmering green tail was surrounded by twenty little girls. Allegra and I sat on the floor, squeezing into the tight circle. We were just in time for pass the parcel, the excited girls passing around the giant newspaper-wrapped parcel while One Direction played in the background. Whenever the music stopped, a layer was unwrapped, revealing a present for each girl. Jemina, the bossy, confident little girl sitting next to us, screamed excitedly when the music stopped and she unwrapped a fluorescent purple hair tie. Allegra was crestfallen; she had hoped it was her turn. The girls around us suddenly became noisier and pressed in tightly, trying to get closer to the mermaid in the middle of the circle. The more the sound bounced off the dark wooden floorboards, the more Allegra burrowed her head into my side. I didn't have a good feeling about where this was heading. Suddenly the little mermaids leapt up, following the Queen Mermaid as she enticed them into a dancing competition on the grass outside. Spotting the purple hair tie left on the floor, I quickly snatched it up, glancing around to check that none of the other mums had seen me stuff it into my pocket.

'Allegra, I've got you that hair elastic.' She slowly turned her face up to me as I stroked her cheek.

'But Mummy, that's not mine—it belongs to Jemima!'

My face flushed pink. I would do anything for my girls, anything to keep them happy, even if it meant stealing another child's pass the parcel prize! Anyway, that Jemima was annoying, far too dominating and assured for such a small person. Her mother was also an expert on everything who was always on time, didn't feed her children sugar, and her house always looked tidy. I was envious of her confidence in a role I was floundering in. What had happened to the part of me that could cope, be in control and be good at something? Harriet often told me that I needed to lower my expectations, about everything from park outings to play dates. I had a tendency to aim for perfection, but my sister was teaching me that by expecting only middling success from small endeavours, any other outcome will be a bonus. Instead of berating myself I needed to celebrate small victories and realise that life with kids often goes pear-shaped. And it hadn't been all bad at the party, I thought as I licked the thick, sweet icing off a slab of birthday cake. While I sat in the car waiting for Allegra to put her belt on, I tucked away an extra lolly bag into my jacket pocket. The freckles would go very nicely with a cup of tea in bed tonight. And I wasn't going to share them with anyone!

I felt sure that if I found my professional groove, managing play dates and kids' birthday parties would be easier. Even though I had recovered from my *Play School* disappointment, I was still eager for that performance buzz. And that was how I found myself in a musical, *Side by Side by Sondheim*, sharing the stage with Margi, my singing teacher, and two other incredible singers. Thankfully for the audience, I narrated the show, and sang only a couple of notes. Every evening as I sat on the stage in the pitch-black, waiting for the spotlight to warm my face, a part of me grew stronger and brighter. All that part needed was a gentle nudge, helped along by Sondheim's lyrics and a warm, funny cast. Our show had a week-long run at the Seymour Centre in Sydney.

'Don't go, Mummy, you can't leave!' Allegra said, her surprisingly strong hands grabbing around my waist and stopping me from getting out the front door.

'I won't be long—it's only four sleeps, and you'll have so much fun with Grandyfrog. You love it when he looks after you. He lets you drink Coke and stay up and watch Harry Potter movies,' I said, wondering why Allegra never gave her father a hard time when he had to travel for work. We were about to tour the Sondheim show well off Broadway, playing to theatres in a couple of country towns in New South Wales and Victoria.

'No one else's mummy goes away. You always go away. You never have time for us.'

'Don't be so ridiculous—I never go away! I'll be back soon. And I'll bring you a present.'

'A puppy?'

'We'll see!'

Each night of the tour, at the time I would usually be dealing with dinner, bath and bed for my girls, I revelled in putting on false eyelashes and slipping into a black sequinned cocktail frock. When I walked out onto the stage, accompanied by the pitch perfect tones of two baby grand pianos and grasping my handheld mic, I knew my butterfly wings were shimmering and, for now, it was my time.

Once my two week music theatre career finished, I was happy to return to *Weekend Sunrise* and my 'freelance' gig reading the news. Although I still wasn't on a contract with Seven I was now the regular newsreader for the weekend show. Hooray! Those Saturday and Sunday mornings belonged just to me. I would almost whoop with delight as I snuck out of my slumbering house, celebrating the four and a half hours I had to myself. I barely drew breath from when I sat down in the make-up chair until I drove out of the security car park, still laughing from the antics of the show. Those crazy few hours with Andrew O'Keefe, Samantha Armytage, Simon Reeve and James Tobin kept me grounded for the rest of the week.

And those weeks could lurch from relatively calm to chaotic, depending on the mood of our family. Allegra had started school and she wasn't happy about it. On day one I imagined her skipping out of the school gates, beaming about the fun of the asphalt playground and her new friends. The reality was a little less sunshiney.

'I don't think I'll go back to school tomorrow.'

'Really? Why not?'

'My teacher is bossy, sitting on the mat is boring, there's too much lining up, and the bell is annoying.'

I wanted to say, 'Welcome to the world, my darling girl,' but I just smiled and said she had to go back the next day.

'But why?'

'Because the government says you have to, and Mummy will get into trouble if you don't go.'

'I think Julia Gillard is stupid . . .'

Each morning I had to use my imagination to get her to school. And if my arsenal of persuasion, negotiation, shouting and strawberry and cream lollies failed, there was always my favourite weapon: bribery, with a capital B. The big gun saved for the end of a tricky week was a visit to the local toy store. I knew that was a big parenting fail, but I had discovered the power of gold star stickers on a reward chart. Even if my mild-mannered husband would rip them up in previously unseen moments of frustration when we couldn't get our daughters to stay in their beds at night.

Logically I knew that part-time work was my salvation and it would be hard, almost impossible, to take on any more work than the *Weekend Sunrise* gig. However, I found it hard to ignore the perverse part of my brain that still sought out challenges, adventure and stimulation. There was also the feeling that I had unfinished business on television, and deep down I wanted another opportunity to show people (mainly myself) who I was and what I was capable of.

My mobile rang one day as I walked home after a fairly successful preschool and school drop-off. It was Rob McKnight, the producer of a new morning show that would be called *Studio 10*. Media icon Ita Buttrose had already been signed up as a co-host along with journalist Joe Hildebrand. I was in awe of Ita, a trailblazer for women, and someone who had balanced a long and varied career with her family. Over the years I had nervously said hello to her, hoping some of her gravitas would rub off on me!

I knew Joe because we had worked together on *Weekend Sunrise*, where he was genius at insightful and controversial commentary. As Rob asked me to audition, for the remaining co-host role, I looked out over the sweep of Sydney Harbour and attempted to sound nonchalant about this exciting opportunity. I winced, hearing the tinge of desperation in my voice as

I asked for the details. Once I hung up, there was no stopping my out-of-control excitement as I imagined myself the new Oprah Winfrey of Australian television. I was going to be big! I was going to make it! When I called my agent, David Wilson, in a spin, he calmed me down and told me to focus on the audition first before making plans for world domination.

The audition went well and I knew I had done my best; secretly, I was really hoping one of the jobs would be mine. During the week that followed, I frequently rang my mobile number from the home phone to check it was still working. So when I recognised the producer's number on the phone a fortnight later, I let it ring a few more times, preparing myself for the good news. However, it was not to be: I was told I wasn't what they were looking for. Instead the fabulous Sarah Harris was the third person to be announced as a co-host of Studio 10. I had met Sarah years before when we both worked at Channel Nine and I loved her warmth and naturalness on air. I stayed civil through the conversation and polite goodbye, then hung up and wailed to my two cats.

Peter held my hand and tried to comfort me as I started to fall into a pathetic mess of self-pity later that evening. My agent, David, was also reassuring and tried to make me feel better by doing a wicked character assassination of my competitors. While I wallowed, Peter secretly hatched a plan with my agent, explaining how much I was struggling to find ongoing, satisfying work after a run of bad luck. And David, also on the sly from me, spoke with the producer and convinced him to give me another shot at an audition for the remaining co-host. I was unaware of what Peter and David had done, and the next thing I knew I had a call from David saying they wanted me to trial again.

When I sat down with Ita, Joe and Sarah on the panel I just went for it, wearing my heart on my sleeve. It was fun: I enjoyed chatting, arguing and questioning them. This time I had nothing to lose and felt calm and secure, simply being myself. It was something I'd never really had permission to do on camera before. As I waved goodbye to the crew I was far more realistic, realising that I probably wouldn't get the job, but it would be okay this time.

Two days later the phone rang. Again I recognised the producer's number, but since I had already convinced myself that it would be better for my family if I didn't get the job, I was just waiting for him to again say thanks but no thanks.

'Hi Jess,' said Rob McKnight.

'Oh, hello.'

'I wanted to call . . .'

I know, to say that you haven't got the job, I thought.

'. . . to tell you that you're our fourth panellist.'

'*What?*'

'You've got the job, Jess. It was a no-brainer.'

'Oh. My. *God!*' I screamed. 'I can't believe it.'

Suddenly things started to look up as I finally returned to full-time work for the first time since I had my girls. Ironically, I was returning to full-time work at Network Ten, the place that had taken me to court all those years ago, but none of the senior executives who had tried to sue me were working there anymore. The familiar faces belonged to the studio cameramen, make-up artists and the receptionist. In a strange way, although so much had changed in my life, when I walked into the studio it was like I was coming home. My job description was to be myself, to laugh, listen and argue for two and a half hours every day on the television. As a panellist on *Studio 10*, I worked with three other fine people and we talked, talked and talked about the big and little issues of the day. It was heaven. I skipped out of the house each morning, my handbag packed with my favourite pink lipstick, a padded Pleasure State bra and my shorthand notebook. I always found bras uncomfortable to wear, especially early in the morning, but I needed the extra padding they gave my flat chest. So I tried to remember to pack one each morning. Sneaking out of the front door just as the cheeky kookaburras were clearing their throats, I felt completely happy for the first time in a long, long time.

Until I had one again, I didn't realise how lost I'd been without a permanent paid job. Working again helped my brainwaves rediscover their silver, zapping rhythms, independent of bedtime dramas, food-strewn highchairs, playground politics and endless routine. But alas, isn't there always a sting in the tail? The obstacle that still occasionally broke my stride was my guilt, a tiny voice that sometimes got a little louder, especially when I was tired. Or when I was unable to do canteen duty, or had forgotten to fill out lunch orders or find lost school shoes.

Despite having managed to lose my self-imposed Wonder Woman crown under the vast collection of Barbies and glitter pens crammed into the pink storage box of my life, I still cannot wipe away my mother guilt. The contradiction, despite relishing going to work each day, that guilty feeling seeps into my soft, mushy heart. Was I depriving my girls because I was not with them 24/7?

'Mummy you're never here. You're always working. Don't leave me,' said Allegra. Her superpower hearing means she has been woken up by the sounds of me creeping down the stairs to make a coffee before going to work.

'That's not true,' I argued gently. 'I pick you up from school every afternoon, I cook your dinner, read you *Diary of a Wimpy Kid* each night . . .'

Why was I justifying my decisions to my seven-year-old daughter? Didn't I get any bonus points for all the years I *was* here when my girls were teeny babies, all day every day?

'Allegra, you're so lucky. Your daddy takes you to school every morning. How many girls have their daddy to do that? How many dads do canteen duty?'

'But I want you to.'

'But Mummy picks you up every afternoon. Not all mummies can do that. And Mummy is lucky because I am doing a job that I love to do.'

Peter works longer hours than I do and he doesn't get daddy guilt! Is there such a thing? How do I make up for this hole? Too often I try to rub away the guilt by being the ultimate Yes Mummy. Yes, we can have sushi, yes, we can have a movie night, yes, have chocolate for breakfast . . .

My guilt is not going to go away. Unfortunately for me, I still put too much pressure on myself to have everything just right. It's an occupational hazard of being a mum. I was also learning that I could have it all, but not at the same time. Yes, I could be a good wife, a good mother, a good daughter, have a career, be ever-present in my children's lives, have close friends—I could have these things, but not every part of my complex life would be perfectly balanced all the time. Priorities would ebb and flow, depending on what stage we were at as a family. Some things would take time, regardless of how much I wanted them right now.

'Mummy, I hate you and your dresses are disgusting.' Ouch, Giselle sure knew how to hurt me. Once my youngest daughter started targeting my favourite leopard-print frock, I knew we were on shaky ground. Some days her words are harder to brush off than others. Today I am sleep-deprived and cranky; even the waterproof glue on my false eyelashes is starting to wilt under the pressure. And again I'm ready to say 'yes' to fill that guilt gap.

'Mummy, will you pick me up early from preschool tomorrow?' Giselle asked.

'Sure thing. I'll get you just before your afternoon tea and we can have some special time before we pick up Allegra from school.'

Bolting from work and a record-breaking trip around the supermarket, I made it to the preschool gates just as the kids were sitting down on miniature plastic chairs to start their afternoon tea of cheese, crackers and cut-up watermelon. I crouched down next to my cherubic child.

'I'm *not* ready to go yet!' Giselle almost growls.

'But . . . but you wanted me to pick you up early, didn't you?'

'This is my favourite part of the day—I'm not going yet.'

I pulled up one of the spare weeny plastic chairs and squished down next to my indignant daughter, waiting for her to be ready to leave. All the time I was thinking, I'm a bad mother—she would rather be here than spending time with me.

Why did I do this to myself? I even sought the wisdom of Ita Buttrose, who had forged an extraordinary career and raised her family at a time when most women stayed at home. I was lucky to sit next to her every day.

'Jessica, guilt means you've done something wrong. You haven't done anything wrong.'

She was right. It might not be for everyone, but I knew it was so right for me: paid, satisfying work had helped me get my sparkle back. And that meant I was going to be the best mummy I could possibly be for Allegra and Giselle because I was happy.

EPILOGUE

Vibrant splashes of purple are appearing in my neighbourhood, the bloom of the jacaranda trees shouting out that summer is on the way. My daughters and I hop over the fallen lilac leafs, careful not to slip on the damp petals.

'Look, Mummy, look!'

'Come on, we need to go!' I'm grumpy, desperate to get home and wipe off my television make-up. The padded underwire bra that I've been wearing all day is digging into my back. I'm busting to rip it off and get changed into my daggy cat-patterned pyjamas. The white plastic shopping bags are starting to slip from my sweaty fingers, packed full of the familiar dinner ingredients of pre-crumbed chicken schnitzel, corn and potatoes. Dinner, bath and bed. It's a moment that I don't want to be in and a moment that I get stuck in every afternoon.

'Oh, it goes in the blink of an eye! Make sure you enjoy every moment,' is a refrain I have often heard from well-meaning older relatives and kind strangers. But I'm still not enjoying every moment, I don't want to be dragged back to the beautiful tree. I want to go home, unpack the shopping bags, and see if I can hide in the toilet for a few minutes of peace.

'I don't like it, I'm not eating it!' says my youngest daughter.

'What do you mean you don't like it? The only thing you eat is schnitzel and mash, and you told me you wanted it for dinner tonight!' I can't hide my exasperation. 'Hey, stop it, don't hit your sister. I don't care who started it. Someone will lose an eye, put that Barbie plane down right now!'

'Mummy, why can't I get my ears pierced?' Allegra begins her evening interrogation. 'Can we have dinner in front of television? Why do I have to go to school? I'm sick, and you shouldn't send a sick child to school. Anyway, I don't need to go to school if I'm going to open my own florist shop!'

'But Mummy,' interjects Giselle, 'I don't want to have legs. I want to be a mermaid.'

'I don't want to be a mermaid, I want to be a boy, so I can marry a princess . . .'

One way of trying to appreciate the little things has been to deliberately lose my mobile once I get home with my girls. It removes the temptation to escape into a parallel universe, even if Peter has to ring me twenty times before I can find it and talk to him. The realisation that I had to kick my phone habit hit me when Allegra told me to get off Twitter one night and play with her.

However, hiding my phone hasn't been enough. More and more I draw on 'mindfulness', a term I had originally discarded as being too hippy because it jarred with my prejudice towards science over the spiritual and 'new age'. I am still a big fan of my antidepressants and taking them each morning, but I've also developed other strategies to help me manage the hurly-burly of my life. I have also learnt there is oodles of science to explain mindfulness, I just had to be prodded in the right direction by my counsellor. Essentially, our clever brains can retrain and rewire themselves to throw out the damaging thoughts that hold us back. For me, I still keep taking those slow deep breaths and focus on either what I can see, feel or taste as a way of short-circuiting those destructive thoughts. And these thoughts that I am not good enough are not true: they are only feelings, not fact.

Taking deep breaths helps bring me into the present more and more.

A small warm hand drags me back to the sandstone fence under the jacaranda tree. My youngest daughter points out a silver lizard that was frozen in the shadow on top of the fence. As we get closer it disappears down the sliver of a crack between the bricks. Suddenly I notice flicker of movement: there is a family of lizards living on this fence. I make a conscious effort to stop, to be here, to be in the right now. And for that moment in time, the present, I am filled with joy.

That same little warm hand takes mine again and again. I can feel the heat and lifeblood radiating up my arm, along my shoulder, down my chest and straight to my heart. Her cat-shaped eyes squint up at me as the warmth of the sun filters through the red bottlebrush trees. I look down at her round, trusting face and feel lighter. It has been a good day.

'Look up through those branches,' I say.

'I know what you're going to say . . .' Giselle begins.

'Oh, come on, you know how much Mummy likes to have a chat. See those two—'

'Birds, I know.'

'I think it must be a mummy and her daughter.'

The rainbow lorikeets squawk loudly to each other.

'See, they like having a chat too.'

As the smaller bird starts dropping crimson seeds onto the footpath, their squawking becomes louder. We can still hear them as we walk slowly down the hill side by side. My long fingers enclose Giselle's hot little hand and I give it a gentle squeeze.

I sing to my baby girl about the sunshine and how much I love her, trying to remember most of the words from 'You Are the Sunshine of my Life'. Giselle sings back to me. It is our song, the song I sang when she was growing inside of me. This time she doesn't tell me to stop singing.

Allegra also wanted to meet the cheeky lorikeets after she gets home from school. We've started leaving out birdseed and cut-up apple to entice them into our backyard. The iridescent orange fur hat almost covers Allegra's blue eyes as she squints up into the tall eucalyptus trees, trying to spot the pair of lorikeets that she and her sister have nicknamed Rainbow and Colourful. Suddenly there is a screech and flash of technicolour feathers and then the two birds perch on her wrist. We laugh into the cool, clear morning air as the lorikeets try to nudge one another out of the way to eat the quarters of green apple in Allegra's outstretched hand.

Allegra again outstretches her hand, this time to lead her grandmother to our spare bedroom. My eldest daughter has already decorated it with flowers (nicked from a vase of ivory roses in the kitchen) and propped them in plastic cups placed haphazardly around the room. A cup of tea she made especially for her grandmother an hour before sits cold on the bedside table. The final touch is Allegra's pink hot water bottle resting on the pillow, placed there after she had decided it was important for her Marmi to stay cosy at night.

'We're here to take your sadness away,' Allegra says to her grandmother, who is shakily trying to unpack her bag.

'My darling, that is such a beautiful thought. We're all here together to help, aren't we?' I say. I can hear a whisper in my heart that says, 'And it's not just your job, Jessica. You are enough, you are good enough.'

We tuck Mum into bed, and I take my daughters to their rooms. Giselle had taken to sleeping on the little mattress on the floor next to her big girl's bed. It used to be her cot mattress, and for a year it has been shoved under her big sister's bed gathering dust. I stroke her light brown hair as she asks for another song.

'Baa, baa, black sheep, have you any woooool . . .'

'Not that one, another one.'

'Mary had a little lamb, little lamb . . .'

'Another one.'

'Ummm . . .'

Giselle begins to sing in a clear, gentle voice. 'Twinkle, twinkle, little star, how I wonder what you are.'

'Now it's time for Mummy to lie with Allegra.'

'You always lie with her for longer.'

'I'll be back to give you a kiss.'

Snuggling against my eldest daughter, I marvel at how tall she has become. Just an hour before I had wrapped her up tightly in the red mermaid bath towel and carried her into the bedroom, the pair of us spinning around and laughing until we couldn't bear it any longer.

Allegra reaches her hand across to me. 'Mummy . . .'

'Mummy's here, darling, Mummy's here.' Half of my body is now off the bed as I kneel on the floor and keep stroking her hair while she goes off to sleep. As her breathing deepens I stand up, ready to sneak out, then trip over a tangle of teddy bears in the doorway of the bedroom. I smile, knowing this is my beautiful, messy, wonderful life. And there is nowhere I would rather be.

ACKNOWLEDGEMENTS

Thank you Patti Miller for giving me the confidence to write from the heart. I wouldn't have had the courage to keep peeling back the layers without you and the glorious group of fellow writers in our Faber Memoir writing course. Big love and gratitude to Annette Barlow, publisher extraordinaire, who has held my hand for years, gently nudging me to get more and more down on the page. Thanks to Anthony Reeder who nursed my manuscript through it's rough and racy early stages. Rebecca Kaiser who patiently and painstakingly has made sure my book makes sense! Andy Palmer for getting my story to the wider world. And to my family and friends, you are what matters most of all. I know that without you I am nothing. Xx